MARTHA ROSE SHULMAN

# Classic Finger Foods & Appetizers

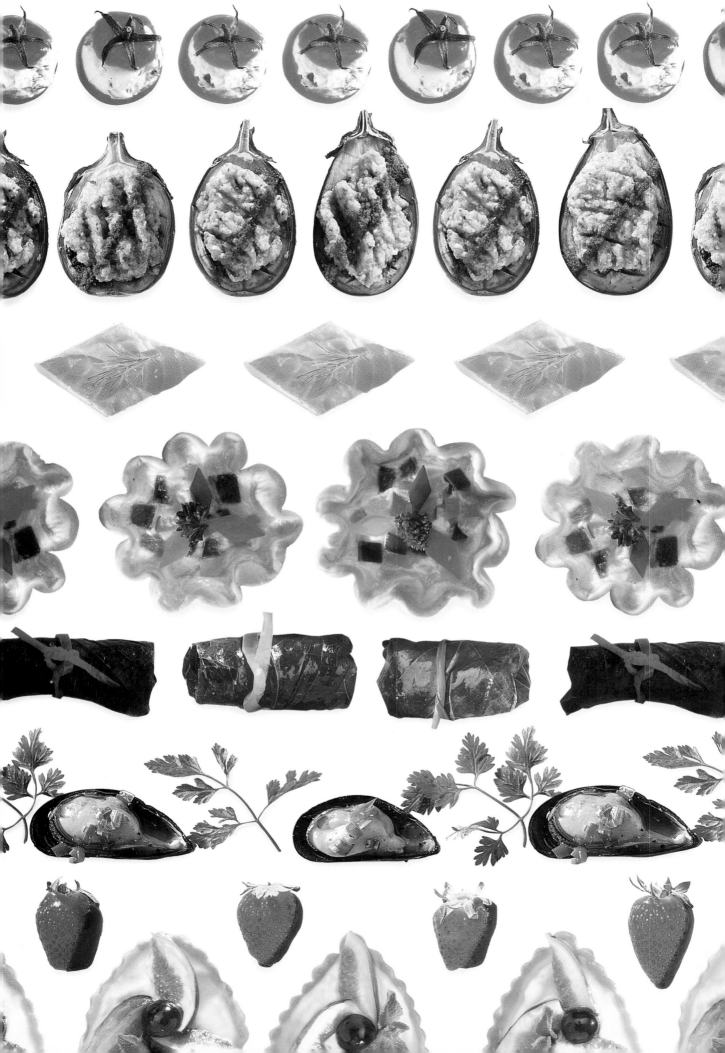

# MARTHA ROSE SHULMAN

# CLASSIC
# FINGER FOODS
# & APPETIZERS

RD
PRESS

MONTREAL

## A DORLING KINDERSLEY BOOK

Created and produced by
CARROLL & BROWN LIMITED
5 Lonsdale Road
London NW6 6RA

**Project Editor** Shirin Patel
**Assistant Editors** Anne Hildyard and Stella Vayne

**Editorial Consultant** Jeni Wright

**Art Direction** Chrissie Lloyd and Louisa Cameron
**Designer** Michael Dyer

**Photography** David Murray and Jules Selmes

**Production** Wendy Rogers and Amanda Mackie

## Food Preparation by Eric Treuillé

Published in Canada in 1995 by
The Reader's Digest Association (Canada) Ltd.
215 Redfern Avenue, Westmount, Quebec H3Z 2V9

The Reader's Digest Association (Canada) Ltd.
is a licensed user of the trademark RD Press

First published in Great Britain in 1995
by Dorling Kindersley Limited,
9 Henrietta Street, London WC2E 8PS
Copyright © 1995 Dorling Kindersley Limited

CANADIAN CATALOGUING IN PUBLICATION DATA
Shulman, Martha Rose
Classic finger foods and appetizers

Includes index.
ISBN 0-88850-325-3

1. Appetizers. 2. Buffets (Cookery).
I. Reader's Digest Association (Canada).
II. Title.

TX740.S59 1995   641.8'12   C95-900003-8

Reproduced by Colourscan, Singapore
Printed and bound in Italy by A. Mondadori, Verona
95 96 97 98 99 / 5 4 3 2 1

# FOREWORD

★

I decided to make a career out of what I loved to do best – cooking and entertaining – one Sunday morning after a huge all-night party I had given. I had spent most of my time that night replenishing the finger foods and appetizers, making sure they looked beautiful so that my guests would feel as if the party might last forever. It was a great party, and afterwards I was absolutely sure that cooking was what I wanted to do.

My Sunday morning decision was not just a whim in a morning-after haze. Within the year, I had launched a catering service and was handling weddings and parties, conferences, and other events. I learned how to cook for large groups. And more than anything, I learned about classic party fare – finger foods and appetizers – because that was the way we usually served our food. We would rent long tables, cover them with colorful cloths, and set out beautiful platters of food. We followed a timetable, which I always drew up once I had decided on a menu.

My purpose here is to help make entertaining as much fun for you as it is for me. The range of delicious possibilities is limitless, and this collection of recipes is just a beginning.

*Martha Rose Shulman*

# CONTENTS

★

## FISH, MEAT, & POULTRY 95

*Here are recipes for a more substantial spread, or for barbecuing outdoors. The fish dishes are light and fresh, pâtés and terrines more satisfying.*

## DESSERTS 113

*Fresh fruit is served with a variety of creams and pastries, while chocolate desserts are the ultimate treat.*

## TECHNIQUES 135

*Review recipes and techniques on which the wide variety of dishes in this collection are based, and gain essential know-how for successful entertaining.*

## AUTHOR'S NOTES 156
## INDEX 157
## ACKNOWLEDGMENTS 160

# INTRODUCTION

★

Whether we entertain on a small or a large scale, formally or informally, today's choice is more often than not a buffet. Serving party fare such as finger foods and tiny appetizers also gives us a wide range of menu choices, either a substantial meal made from several dishes, or a few delicate morsels to precede a meal.

The foods we are likely to serve are a far cry from the predictable canapés of yesteryear. Today our menus are light, colorful, and eclectic, with strong, ethnic flavors. So, besides gougères, quiches, and terrines, our party table is likely to include Italian toasted country bread with garlic and olive oil and topped with an assortment of robust vegetable mixtures, crisp Middle Eastern phyllo pastries, buckwheat blini with smoked salmon, and gingery spring rolls filled with shrimp and cilantro. We might also find platters of spicy Mexican nachos or Japanese inspired sushi rolls, as well as Indonesian style saté.

These days we seem to have less time than ever, so if we want to cook and entertain, we have to find ways to save time without sacrificing quality. That's why you'll find many recipes here for dishes such as frittatas and pizzas that can be made in one large pan, then cut into bite-sized portions. There are also plenty of suggestions for ready-made items that can be used as fillings and toppings. For example, a good bottled pesto can be spread on crostini and topped with a cooked shrimp or scallop, then garnished with a fresh herb sprig for a beautiful hors d'oeuvre that can be assembled in minutes. You'll find time-saving tips like this throughout the book.

Today's buffets also reflect our growing concern with health and our newfound appreciation of fresh produce. Appetizers used to be filled with high-fat calories — nuts and cheese, chips served with sour-cream-based dips, vol-au-vents, and fried foods. Today, guests want lighter choices. Although this collection includes some high-protein dishes (the terrines, pâtés, and fish, for example), the greater number of recipes are based on fresh vegetables and low-fat fish,

*Aïoli Platter*

poultry, and meat, such as seviche and saté. This doesn't mean that they are not substantial. Colorful omelets filled with red peppers and fresh peas or spinach and fresh herbs, nachos topped with shredded chicken and green tomatillo salsa or black beans, pungent, gingery tuna and eggplant kebabs are all extremely satisfying, but they won't make your guests feel that they have overindulged.

Desserts can also have a prominent place on a buffet table, and sometimes an entire party can be focused on them. The dessert recipes in this volume are a good balance of rich and light ingredients and flavors. Fruit, the dessert equivalent of crudités, is ever present in tartlets, and on platters with creamy dips.

*Lamb Terrine en Gelée*

## Planning a Party

Organizing a party is like planning for an opening night. Your party table will be your set, and curtain time will be when the guests arrive. When it's all over, you will dismantle the set – clear the table, load the dishwasher, and start cleaning up. Stage fright is often part of the bargain. Indeed, friends often tell me that they never enjoy their own parties.

But you can have a good time at your own party if you plan carefully. When planning the menu, consider the time available to you and the amount of help you will have. If these are limited, don't plan to serve many time-consuming items such as those that must be wrapped or rolled. Instead, make whole frittatas and savory quiches and cut them into bite-sized servings. Choose items that can be made in advance and frozen, such as blini or phyllo pastries. Serve platters of crudités with dips, bearing in mind that most crudités can be cut up in advance and kept in the refrigerator overnight. Have a mix of hot and cold dishes.

For dessert, you could buy petits fours to serve with bowls of fruit. Sometimes I set out a huge basket of tangerines with an assortment of chocolates, small cookies, and unsalted nuts.

*Spinach &
Feta Cheese
phyllo pastry*

## Choosing a Theme

Party food can have a theme – Italian, Mexican, or Middle Eastern, for example – or you can have an assortment of dishes from different countries. It's advisable not to serve too many different types of ethnic food at the same time, however. For instance, if you are serving several Asian dishes, it's best not to serve nachos as well. Delicately seasoned dishes such as quiches, frittatas, or carpaccios won't clash with finger foods that have more pronounced flavors, such as kebabs and meatballs.

Appetizers as a prelude to a meal need not be very elaborate: a few tasty items will do, and these should not be too filling. If the dishes are for a cocktail or evening party they should be more substantial, because they may well be a substitute for dinner. For such an occasion, have five or more dishes, with a balance of protein-rich, vegetable, and high-carbohydrate items. Serve one or two kinds of savory quiches or omelets, a pâté or a selection of meatballs or perhaps seviche, stuffed vegetables or a platter of vegetable crudités with dips, bruschetta, and a platter of phyllo pastries. Party food should be easy to handle. Serve items that can be eaten with one hand in a couple of bites, but provide places for guests to set down their drinks just in case they need to use their other hand to deal with food.

*Chicken nachos*

### Hot or Cold?

Whether you include hot food at your party depends in part on how substantial the selection is meant to be. I dislike chafing dishes (except for the very simple Bagna Cauda, which must be kept hot), because the food can become soggy. When I serve hot food, it is usually the type that is baked, then served straight from the oven, such as phyllo pastries or mushrooms filled with pesto.

It is easier to deal with hot food if you have help in the kitchen: you can host the party while your helpers watch the oven. However, as most of the dishes in this collection can be served at room temperature, you can choose only these for your party, if you cannot have help.

### Arranging the Table

Food should look colorful and enticing on a party table. Use attractive platters, plates, baskets, and bowls for displaying food, and garnish foods that are not naturally bright in color with sprigs of fresh herbs, radish roses, cherry tomatoes, chilis, or lemon or lime wedges.

I like to pass around some of the dishes on smaller plates and platters, so that guests don't have to crowd around the party table. If space is limited, you can fit a large number of items on a table if you alternate platters and plates in a zigzag pattern. Put out knives to spread foods such as hummus and pâtés, and arrange napkins within easy reach of dishes such as stuffed vegetables and dips.

Since platters should look as if they have just been set out, they should be replenished as soon as they are half empty – bring out replacements on smaller plates. Regularly remove empty bottles, paper plates, and full ashtrays.

### Organization

The key to successful entertaining is planning. Once you have decided on your menu, make lists. I make two lists when I entertain – a shopping list and a calendar – with the menu written at the top and all the tasks assigned to their particular days. If the party is a very large one, I may also make a list of equipment and serving dishes and utensils I know I will need.

I try to begin as far ahead of time as possible. If there is something that can be frozen, for instance, pizza crust or pastry for quiches and tartlets, blini, and phyllo pastries, I will make it

*Mini Fruit Sandwiches*

at least a week in advance. Dishes that can be frozen are often time-consuming items to make, so it's good to prepare them beforehand.

I try to do all the shopping by the day of the party; the exception is, of course, fresh fish or raw meats for marinating, but these items can be ordered, so all I have to do is to pick them up. I also set up my party table and bar and arrange flowers the night before. There is something comforting about the room looking ready well in advance.

## A Party Checklist

Decide the date and time

Plan guest list

Send out invitations

Plan menu

Check recipes to make in advance
   and freeze

Assess space, tables, chairs

Assess number of dishes, glasses,
   plates, cutlery, and serving dishes

Make shopping list for
   food and drinks (including
   coffee and tea)

Make ice

Prepare dishes

Chill wine

Arrange flowers

Arrange table

## Tips for Storing Food

Storing food in limited refrigerator space can be tricky, but the more that can be stored, the more can be prepared in advance. Plastic bags are space savers. Except for raw carrots, celery, and radishes, which must be kept in cold water, cut-up raw vegetables and blanched and steamed vegetables can be sealed in plastic bags. To keep herbs fresh, cut the stems off about ¼ in (5 mm) from the ends, wrap the ends of the stems in dampened paper towels, and then wrap them tightly in foil. Seal in a plastic bag. Cheese can be shredded and bagged. Store dips and spreads in jars in the refrigerator door, or in containers that can be stacked. To store prepared platters of food, stand corks on the platters so that their tops are higher than the surface of the food, and cover: the corks will hold the covering off the food.

## Quantities and Quantity Cooking

I always count on guests having at least 2–3 items of each dish at a buffet. Most of the recipes in this book serve 10 people, and some serve up to 20. All the recipes can be multiplied to serve larger groups, but remember to allow more time for preparation, even for simple dishes. If you are serving individual wrapped and rolled items or are having more than 10 guests, I recommend that you enlist someone to help you. Knowing that there will be somebody to assist with preparation, serving, and keeping it all looking good will help you relax and enjoy your own party even more.

# DRINKS

★

A glass of chilled white or sparkling wine or a cocktail will get any party off to a good start and help guests to relax. When entertaining, it is a good idea to have plenty of alcoholic and nonalcoholic drinks. However, you will find serving and refilling easier if there is a limited choice. If you can, buy more than is needed and arrange to return what is left over.

### Cool and Collected

Keep in mind some practical considerations. Make sure there are plenty of corkscrews and bottle openers so that more than one person can open drinks. Plenty of ice is essential: make it in advance or buy it ready-made. When the weather is cold, wines can be stored outside to chill; otherwise, if space in the refrigerator is limited, bottles can be kept cool in the bathtub or in buckets filled with ice and water.

### Separate Tables

Arrange a separate table for drinks so that the food tables don't get too crowded. It helps if someone is in charge of serving drinks, at least initially. Or have glasses of wine or champagne ready to offer around on a tray.

### Happy Hour

When guests arrive, welcome them with an aperitif, such as kir, made with crème de cassis (black currant liqueur) and a dry white wine; mint julep; champagne; or mimosa. Once food is served, offer a choice of chilled white wine, red wine, or punch. Your choice of wine will be determined by factors such as your budget, your personal preferences, or the type of food that is being served.

### Wine Choice

In general, for cocktail parties, sparkling wines, white wines such as Chardonnay and Sancerre, or light reds such as Fleurie or Valpolicella are very acceptable. For brunches, mimosas are ideal. At lunch time, pick light wines, such as Vinho Verde, Bordeaux, or a dry rosé. With a meaty meal, choose full-bodied reds such as Chianti, Barolo, or a Cabernet Sauvignon.

### Specialty Drinks

For the themed parties suggested in this book, it is fun to serve an appropriate drink:

**Middle Eastern Mezze:** Buzbag (a full-bodied Turkish red wine), Arak (an anise-flavored aperitif) or Turkish coffee.
**A French Buffet:** Kir or Kir Royale, Noilly Prat, or Dubonnet.
**Celebrating Italy:** Martini, Campari, Punt e Mes, Frascati, or Soave.
**A Feast from Asia:** Rice wine, beer, jasmine or orange pekoe tea.
**A Mexican Fiesta:** Tequila or Margaritas.
**A Summer Party:** Mint julep, Summer Fruit Punch, or Piña Colada Punch (see page 13).

Cocktails that often taste deceptively light can actually be quite lethal in their effect, so it is best to be judicious about mixing spirits.

Have a good stock of nonalcoholic drinks, such as soda water, tomato juice, carbonated and still mineral waters, cola, and fruit juices.

## Average Drink Quantities

| Drink | 1 person | 10 people | 20 people | 50 people |
| --- | --- | --- | --- | --- |
| Wine | ½ bottle | 5 bottles | 10 bottles | 25 bottles |
| Punch or Mulled Wine | ½ cup/125 ml | 5 cups/1.25 liters | 5 pints/3 liters | 6 quarts/6 liters |
| Sparkling wine or champagne | 1 cup/250 ml | 4 bottles | 8 bottles | 20 bottles |
| Mimosa: champagne | ¼ cup/60 ml | 1¼ bottles | 2½ bottles | 6 bottles |
| orange juice | ¼ cup/60 ml | 2½ cups/600 ml | 5 cups/1.25 liters | 3 quarts/3 liters |
| Hard liquor | 2½ fl oz/75 ml | 1 bottle | 2 bottles | 5 bottles |

**A PRETTY PUNCH**
*Serve chilled Summer Party Punch in a bowl that highlights the colors of the wine and the fruit.*

# SUMMER PARTY PUNCH

*Makes about 2¹/2 quarts (2.5 liters)*

### INGREDIENTS

*1 lb (500 g) dessert apples, sliced
1 cup (250 ml) orange liqueur
¹/2 cup (125 ml) cognac
1 orange, thinly sliced
1 lemon, thinly sliced
2 cups (250 g) strawberries, sliced
3 bottles of sparkling wine
ice cubes
mint and lemon verbena sprigs for decoration*

### PREPARATION

1 Put the apple slices in a large punch bowl. Stir in the liqueur and cognac. Cover and chill in the refrigerator for at least 2 hours.
2 Add the orange and lemon slices to the bowl about 1 hour before serving.
3 Just before serving, add the strawberries, sparkling wine, and ice cubes. Mix well and decorate with mint and lemon verbena sprigs.

# MULLED WINE

*Makes about 6¹/2 quarts (6.5 liters)*

### INGREDIENTS

*2 quarts (2 liters) water
1¹/4 lb (625 g) sugar
6 cloves
2 cinnamon sticks
2 lemons, thinly sliced
peeled zest of 1 lemon
6 bottles red wine, such as Burgundy or claret
lemon slices to decorate*

### PREPARATION

1 Bring the water, sugar, and spices to a boil in a large pan. Add the lemon slices and lemon zest, stir well, and let stand for 10 minutes or until the sugar has dissolved.
2 Add the red wine and warm through: do not boil.
3 Strain into a warmed punch bowl and serve hot, decorated with lemon slices.

# PINA COLADA PUNCH

*The popular West Indian cocktail of pineapple and cream of coconut is here converted to a lighter punch.*
*Makes about 5 quarts (5 liters)*

### INGREDIENTS

*3 tbsp brown sugar
2-in (5-cm) piece dried ginger root, crushed
2¹/2 cups (600 ml) cold water
¹/2 lb (250 g) dehydrated coconut
1¹/4 quarts (1.25 liters) boiling water
2¹/2 cups (600 ml) dark rum
2¹/2 quarts (2.5 liters) pineapple juice
cocktail cherries, pineapple chunks, and ice to decorate*

### PREPARATION

1 Put the sugar, ginger, and the cold water in a pan, bring to a boil, and simmer for 1–2 minutes. Let cool and strain into a serving bowl.
2 Meanwhile, mix together the coconut and boiling water in another pan and let stand for 10 minutes.
3 Strain the coconut mixture into the serving bowl and mix well. Stir in the rum and pineapple juice and chill for at least 2 hours. Serve decorated with cocktail cherries, pineapple chunks, and ice.

# Menu Planning

Whatever the occasion, large or small, informal or formal, indoors or out, a buffet-style party with a range of finger foods and appetizers is ideal. Here are some menu suggestions for different types of entertaining.

★

# JUST ONE COURSE

Appetizers and finger foods are very adaptable. They can make up the whole of a meal or just a part of it. For a simple menu, serve a selection of only savory or sweet dishes.

## JUST STARTERS

★

Smoked Trout Deviled Eggs (page 42)

Herbed Goat Cheese Crêpes (page 54)

Roast Pepper & Mozzarella Crostini (page 70)

Shrimp & Tomato Nachos (page 82)

Mussels on the Half Shell (page 102)

Lamb Terrine en Gelée (page 112)

★

## JUST DESSERTS

★

Fresh Fruit Tartlets (page 114)

Rich Pecan Squares (page 118)

Coffee Cream Puffs (page 120)

Celebration Brownies (page 124)

Biscotti with Raisins (page 126)

Mini Fruit Sandwiches (page 130)

Summer Fruit Platter (page 132)

★

**Lamb Terrine en Gelée**          **Fresh Fruit Tartlets**

# COCKTAIL PARTIES

One of the easiest ways to entertain a large number of guests is at a cocktail party. The menus are interchangeable for a luncheon or an evening party. The weather may dictate whether hot or cold appetizers should be served, but whichever are chosen, it is always best to serve plenty of tidbits with drinks, and to include some which are high in protein.

## COLD SPREAD

★

*Seviche*

*Baba Ghanouj (page 30)*

*Aïoli Platter (page 32)*

*Tender Pea & Pepper Frittata (page 39)*

*Olive Focaccia (page 67)*

*Rice & Meat Dolmades (page 78)*

*Chicken Nachos with Salsa Verde (page 83)*

*Seviche (page 104)*

*Almond Biscotti (page 126)*

★

## HOT SPREAD

★

*Blini with Corn & Tomato Salsa (page 47)*

*Spinach Quiche (page 58)*

*Wild Mushroom & Herb Pizza (page 65)*

*Anchovy Bruschetta (page 71)*

*Leek & Feta Cheese Phyllo Pastries (page 77)*

*Spinach & Tofu Wontons (page 88)*

*Shrimp & Pepper Kebabs (page 98)*

*Rhubarb & Honey Tartlets (page 116)*

★

*Rhubarb & Honey Tartlets*

# BRUNCH & LUNCH

An informal brunch or lunch is an ideal opportunity for relaxed entertaining. Midmorning brunch combines the best of breakfast and lunch, and a selection of New Wave dishes, such as frittata and sushi, will add a stylish touch. For lunch, choose more substantial dishes, such as the hot dip, Bagna Cauda, or Chicken & Pepper Kebabs.

## ELEGANT BRUNCH

★

*Smoked Salmon & Dill Frittata (page 38)*

*Tapenade Deviled Eggs (page 43)*

*Blini with Caviar & Fromage Blanc (page 46)*

*Platter of Quiches (page 58)*

*Wild Mushroom Bruschetta (page 72)*

*Cucumber Sushi (page 84)*

*Cherry Clafoutis Tartlets (page 119)*

★

## LIGHT LUNCH

★

*Bagna Cauda (page 30)*

*Herb & Scallion Quiche (page 58)*

*Sage & Onion Focaccia (page 67)*

*Lamb & Green Vegetable Phyllo Pastries (page 77)*

*Black Bean Nachos (page 82)*

*Crunchy Tofu Soft Spring Rolls (page 92)*

*Chicken & Pepper Kebabs (page 98)*

*Fresh Fruit & Cream Puffs (page 120)*

★

**Platter of Quiches**

**Fresh Fruit & Cream Puffs**

# DINNER PARTIES

Whether entertaining family, friends, or business associates,
a dinner party should be fairly substantial, and when it
consists of finger foods, there should be 2–3 of each item per
guest. If the celebration is on a grander scale, many dishes
can be prepared in advance to make the whole affair
as stylish as possible.

## SPECIAL OCCASION DINNER

★

*Blini with Smoked Salmon & Fromage Blanc
(page 46)*

*Fresh Herb Crostini (page 70)*

*Chicken Nachos with Salsa Verde (page 83)*

*Chicken & Pepper Kebabs (page 98)*

*Clams on the Half Shell (page 102)*

*Lemon Sablés (page 127)*

*Chocolate Meringues (page 130)*

★

**Clams on the Half Shell**

## BUFFET FOR 50

★

*3 recipes Aïoli Platter (page 34)*

*4 recipes Asparagus Frittata (page 39)*

*3 recipes Smoked Trout Deviled Eggs
(page 42)*

*50 Blini with Green Tomatillo Salsa (page 47)*

*2 recipes Chicken Provençal Gougères
(page 51)*

*3 recipes Zucchini & Red Pepper Quiche
(page 58)*

*3 recipes Tomato
& Olive Bruschetta (page 70)*

*4 recipes Tuna & Red Pepper Kebabs
with Ginger-Soy Marinade (page 99)*

*3 recipes Gravadlax (page 104)*

*2 recipes Cranberry-Pear
Tartlets (page 119)*

*2 recipes Fresh Fruit
& Cream Puffs (page 120)*

*1 recipe Ginger Biscotti (page 126)*

*2 recipes Chocolate Fancies (page 130)*

★

# EATING ALFRESCO

Food always tastes better eaten outdoors. Dishes can be
prepared in advance and transported with a minimum of fuss, if
properly packaged. Take advantage of the location
and have a barbecue. If the party is to be held nearer home, in a
garden or around a pool, you can include hot food
ready from the kitchen.

## PACK & GO
★

*Herb Potpourri Deviled Eggs (page 42)*

*Goat Cheese & Pepper Gougères (page 50)*

*Olive Focaccia (page 67)*

*Rice & Herb Dolmades (page 78)*

*California Sushi (page 84)*

*Smoked Duck Soft Spring Rolls
(page 93)*

*Chocolate Chip Cookies (page 127)*

*Lemon Sablés (page 127)*

★

## GARDEN OR POOL PARTY
★

*Zucchini & Red Pepper Frittata (page 38)*

*Blue Cheese & Pear Gougères
(page 50)*

*Asian style Crab Crêpes (page 52)*

*Tomato & Caper Bruschetta
(page 71)*

*Beef & Chicken Saté (page 98)*

*Middle Eastern Meatballs (page 99)*

*Raspberry Clafoutis Tartlets (page 119)*

*Mexican Fruit Platter (page 132)*

★

**Soft & Crispy Spring Rolls**

**Mexican Fruit Platter**

# VEGETABLES

*I don't think I've ever given a party without including
vegetables in some form. They may make up an
attractive platter of crudités with one or more dips
or I serve just a few, such as cucumbers and red
peppers, with a hummus or smoked trout filling.
Vegetarian dishes can be truly exciting, given the wide
variety of exotic and familiar vegetables that is now
available, and the range of flavors I have included.
Stuff mushrooms with pesto, fill cherry tomatoes
with herbed goat cheese, or serve baby new
potatoes with caviar.*

# STUFFED VEGETABLES

No matter how you serve vegetables, they always provide a party table with a colorful focus. Raw vegetables stuffed with a variety of fillings provide contrasting and refreshing textures. I usually pipe the stuffing into the vegetable containers, but you can also spoon it in, as shown in the picture here, if you find this easier.

**A FEAST OF VEGETABLES**
*On the platter are Zucchini Boats filled with Tunisian Zucchini Purée and garnished with a sprinkling of paprika, Tomato Cups filled with Green Olive & Almond Tapenade and garnished with sliced olives and chopped herbs, and Cucumber Rings filled with Tzatziki and garnished with dill.*

## To Make Stuffed Vegetables

*2 cups (500 ml) stuffing fills approximately 2 lb (1 kg) vegetables*

**1** Choose vegetables for stuffing from those suggested on page 25. See also page 148.

**2** Make the raw vegetables into containers by simply hollowing them out for cups or boats, or by blanching or cooking them before shaping, as directed on page 148.

**3** Prepare your choice of stuffing from the recipes given on pages 22–25. Chill the stuffing until you are ready to fill the vegetable containers.

**4** Spoon or pipe the stuffing into the vegetable containers. If serving the stuffed vegetables warm, heat through in a 400°F (200°C) oven for 10 –15 minutes.

*Baby eggplant halves filled with Tunisian Zucchini Purée and sprinkled with paprika*

# STUFFINGS FOR VEGETABLES

*The textures and colors of stuffings should complement their vegetable containers. For maximum variety, mix and match the recipes below with suitable vegetables (see pages 25 and 148).*

★

## GREEN OLIVE & ALMOND TAPENADE

*This is a lighter – and somewhat unorthodox – version of the olive paste named after the Provençal for caper – tapéno. Traditionally, it contains anchovy and tuna, but I have omitted the fish and added almonds.*
*Makes 2 cups (500 ml)*

### INGREDIENTS

*2 large garlic cloves, peeled*
*2 cups (250 g) green Provençal or Greek olives, pitted*
*¼ cup (30 g) almonds*
*1½ tbsp capers, drained and rinsed*
*1 tsp fresh thyme leaves, or ½ tsp dried thyme*
*1 tsp chopped fresh rosemary,*
*or ½ tsp crumbled dried rosemary*
*3 tbsp olive oil*
*2 tbsp lemon juice*
*freshly ground black pepper*

### PREPARATION

**1** Turn on a food processor fitted with the metal blade, and drop in the garlic. When it is chopped, turn off the machine and add the olives, almonds, capers, thyme, and rosemary. Turn on the machine, and process until fairly smooth.
**2** Add the olive oil and lemon juice, and continue processing until the mixture forms a uniform paste. Add pepper to taste.

### Making Tapenade by Hand

*Tapenade can be made using a mortar and pestle instead of a food processor. Pound together the garlic, olives, almonds, and capers. Add the herbs, pound to a paste, and slowly add the olive oil, 1 tbsp at a time, pounding the mixture after each addition. Slowly blend in the lemon juice, 1 tbsp at a time. Add pepper to taste.*

## TZATZIKI

*This pungent mixture of cucumber, yogurt, and garlic is especially good as a filling for beets, red peppers, and cucumbers, but in Greece, where the recipe originated, it is more often used as a dip for pita bread.*
*Makes 3½–4 cups (875 ml–1 liter)*

### INGREDIENTS

*1 cucumber, peeled, and very finely chopped or grated*
*salt and freshly ground pepper*
*2 cups (500 ml) drained yogurt (see page 156)*
*3 garlic cloves, crushed*
*2 tbsp lemon juice*

### PREPARATION

**1** Toss the cucumber with a generous amount of salt and let stand in a colander for 1 hour. Rinse under cold water and squeeze dry.
**2** Beat the yogurt in a bowl with a whisk until smooth. Stir in the cucumber, garlic, lemon juice, and salt and pepper to taste.

## CAVIAR

*The better the quality of caviar you use (see box page 46), the more luxurious this stuffing will be.*
*Makes 1 cup (250 ml)*

### INGREDIENTS

*½ cup (125 ml) fromage blanc (see page 156), plain nonfat yogurt, or sour cream*
*½ cup (125 g) black caviar*

### PREPARATION

**1** Fill each vegetable container with fromage blanc, yogurt, or sour cream.
**2** Top with ½ heaping tsp of caviar.

# TUNISIAN ZUCCHINI PUREE

*This stuffing uses* harissa, *a very hot, North African paste made from chilis, garlic, cumin, coriander, and caraway seeds. It is available in small cans and tubes from delicatessens and Middle Eastern specialty stores. Always use harissa with caution — it is fiery.*
*Makes 3 cups (750 ml)*

## INGREDIENTS

*1 lb (500 g) zucchini, sliced*
*2 large garlic cloves, crushed using a mortar and pestle or garlic press*
*2 tbsp olive oil*
*3/4 tsp ground caraway seeds*
*1/4 tsp harissa or 1/8 tsp cayenne pepper*
*2—4 tbsp lemon juice*
*salt and freshly ground pepper*

## PREPARATION

1 Steam the zucchini for 10–15 minutes, until they are thoroughly tender. Drain and rinse under cold water.
2 Squeeze out as much moisture as possible from the zucchini, and transfer to a food processor fitted with the metal blade. Process until smooth.
3 Add the remaining ingredients to the food processor, with lemon juice, salt, and pepper to taste. Process until evenly mixed, then taste, and adjust seasonings.

 *If you make this zucchini stuffing several hours in advance, reserve the lemon juice and add it shortly before serving. If it is added in advance, it will spoil the bright green color of the zucchini.*

*Harissa*

# BRANDADE

*Brandade is a salt cod purée from France. It makes a tasty filling for tomatoes and peppers.*
*Makes 2 cups (500 ml)*

## INGREDIENTS

*1 lb (500 g) salt cod, dried or fresh*
*2 quarts (2 liters) water*
*2 medium onions, quartered*
*5 large garlic cloves, 3 cut in half, 2 finely chopped*
*2 bay leaves*
*3/4 cup (175 ml) milk*
*1/4 cup (60 ml) olive oil*
*freshly ground pepper*

## PREPARATION

1 Desalt the fish: Place in a large bowl and cover with water. If convenient, put the bowl in the kitchen sink and keep the water running in a thin stream so that the water in the bowl is constantly renewing itself. If this is not convenient, change the soaking water several times over 48 hours for dried salt cod, or over 24 hours for fresh salt cod.
2 Cut the cod into a few large pieces and place in a heavy-bottomed saucepan. Add the water, onions, halved garlic cloves, and the bay leaves. Bring slowly to a simmer over medium-low heat.
3 As soon as the water reaches a simmer and before it comes to a boil, cover the pan, and turn off the heat. Let stand for 10 minutes. Drain the fish and transfer to a bowl. Let stand until cool enough to handle.
4 Remove the bones and skin from the fish. Flake the flesh by rubbing it between your fingers or using a fork or wooden spoon, and check for any hidden small bones. Transfer to a food processor fitted with the metal blade.
5 Scald the milk in a small saucepan, remove from the heat, and add half the olive oil.
6 Heat the remaining oil in a heavy-bottomed saucepan over medium-low heat and add the finely chopped garlic. As soon as it begins to sizzle, remove the pan from the heat, and transfer the garlic and oil to the food processor.
7 Turn on the food processor and add the milk and oil mixture in a slow stream, until the cod has absorbed all the liquid it can. Continue to process until the cod mixture is fluffy, adding pepper to taste.

*Tomato Cups (page 148) stuffed with Herbed Goat Cheese*

## HERBED GOAT CHEESE

*This recipe can also be used as a dip or topping.*
*It will keep for a few hours in the refrigerator.*
*Makes about 2 cups (500 ml)*

### INGREDIENTS

1/2 lb (250 g) nonfat cottage cheese
1/2 lb (250 g) goat cheese
4–6 tbsp (60–90 ml) plain nonfat yogurt
2 garlic cloves, finely chopped or crushed
1 cup (30 g) fresh herbs, such as parsley, tarragon, basil,
dill, chives, chervil, or oregano, finely chopped
salt and freshly ground pepper

### PREPARATION

Combine the cheeses, 4 tbsp (60 ml) yogurt, and
the garlic in a food processor fitted with the metal
blade. Process until smooth, adding more yogurt if
desired. Transfer to a bowl and stir in the herbs,
salt if necessary, and pepper to taste.

## GOAT CHEESE
## WITH SUN-dried TOMATO

*Use this stuffing to top blini (see pages 44–47) and*
*fill crêpes (see pages 52–53).*
*It will keep for up to 3 days in the refrigerator.*
*Makes about 2 cups (500 ml)*

### INGREDIENTS

1/2 lb (250 g) nonfat cottage cheese
1/2 lb (250 g) goat cheese
4–6 tbsp (60–90 ml) plain nonfat yogurt
2 garlic cloves, finely chopped or crushed
3 oz (90 g) oil-packed sun-dried tomatoes, drained
and chopped
salt and freshly ground pepper

### PREPARATION

Combine the cheeses, 4 tbsp (60 ml) yogurt, and
garlic in a food processor fitted with the metal
blade. Process until smooth, adding more yogurt
if desired. Transfer to a bowl and stir in the
sun-dried tomatoes, and salt and pepper to taste.

## NORTH AFRICAN STYLE TUNA

*Mint and cumin lend an exotic flavor to this stuffing.*
*It will keep for 1 day in the refrigerator.*
*Makes about 2 cups (500 ml)*

### INGREDIENTS

2 x 6 1/8-oz (173-g) cans water-packed tuna, drained
2 shallots or 1 bunch scallions, both white and green parts,
finely chopped
1/4 – 1/2 cup (60–125 ml) plain nonfat yogurt
1/4 cup (60 ml) lemon juice
2 garlic cloves, finely chopped or crushed
4 tbsp chopped fresh mint
1/2 tsp ground cumin
salt and freshly ground pepper

### PREPARATION

Break up the tuna into flakes and mash with a fork.
Mix in the remaining ingredients, using the smaller
amount of yogurt first. The mixture should be
fairly smooth. Add more yogurt as desired. Taste,
and adjust seasonings.

## SMOKED TROUT PUREE

*It couldn't be simpler to purée the smoked trout with*
*the other ingredients in a food processor. All you need is*
*excellent smoked trout — pink salmon trout makes the*
*prettiest purée. It will keep for up to 3 days*
*in the refrigerator.*
*Makes about 1 1/4 cups (325 ml)*

### INGREDIENTS

1/2 lb (250 g) smoked trout
1/4 cup (60 ml) plain nonfat yogurt
or fromage blanc (see page 156)
2–3 tbsp lemon juice
1 tbsp crème fraîche
1 tsp Dijon mustard
salt and freshly ground pepper

### PREPARATION

Remove any skin and bones from the trout. Break
the flesh into pieces, place in a food processor
fitted with the metal blade, and process. Add the
remaining ingredients except the salt, adjust the
lemon juice to taste, and process until smooth.
Taste, and add salt if necessary.

# BASIL PESTO

*Pesto isn't just for pasta. Use it to stuff vegetable containers such as cherry tomatoes and mushrooms.*
*Makes about ³⁄4 cup (175 ml)*

### INGREDIENTS

*2 large garlic cloves, peeled*
*2 tbsp pine nuts*
*2 cups (60 g) fresh basil*
*¹⁄4–¹⁄2 tsp salt*
*6 tbsp (90 ml) olive oil*
*¹⁄2 cup (60 g) freshly grated Parmesan cheese*
*2 tbsp grated Pecorino cheese*
*freshly ground pepper*

### PREPARATION

1 Turn on a food processor fitted with the metal blade and drop in the garlic. When it is chopped, turn off the machine, and add the pine nuts, basil, and salt to taste. Turn on the machine and blend together. With the machine running, add the olive oil. Process until the mixture is smooth, stopping the machine from time to time to wipe any basil leaves down from the side of the bowl.
2 Add the cheeses and pepper to taste and mix together well.

### VARIATION

**CILANTRO PESTO:** Substitute *2 cups (60 g) cilantro* for the basil, or a combination of *1 cup (30 g) cilantro, ¹⁄2 cup (15 g) fresh basil,* and *¹⁄2 cup (15 g) flat-leaf parsley.*

 *Pesto freezes well. Process the herbs with the pine nuts, salt, and olive oil. Do not add the garlic, cheeses, or pepper until you defrost the pesto.*

## Making Pesto by Hand

*Both Basil and Cilantro Pesto can be made using a mortar and pestle instead of a food processor. Pound together the garlic and pine nuts. Add the herbs and salt, pound to a paste, and slowly add the olive oil, 1 tbsp at a time, blending it into the mixture after each addition. Blend in the cheeses and adjust seasonings to taste.*

## Vegetable Containers

*Many vegetables, in addition to those shaped into containers on page 148, lend themselves to becoming colorful and complementary receptacles for stuffings.*

**BABY SQUASH BOWLS:** *Cut baby squash in half crosswise and blanch in a pan of boiling salted water. Carefully scoop out some flesh, leaving a ¹⁄2-in (1-cm) border all around.*
**PEPPER CUPS:** *Cut each pepper in half crosswise. Remove the core and scoop out the seeds.*
**SNOW PEA PURSES:** *Blanch snow peas in a large pan of boiling salted water. Carefully slit open the curved side of each pod.*
**BABY BEET CUPS:** *Cook scrubbed beets in boiling salted water for 20–30 minutes. Drain and let cool. Peel and trim. Cut a very thin slice off each beet base so that the beets stand upright. Hollow out each beet with a melon baller or cut out a conical shape with a sharp knife.*
**MUSHROOM CUPS:** *To prepare the mushrooms for baking with a stuffing in them, simply twist off the stems, and rinse or wipe the caps. If the mushrooms are to have a cold stuffing, place them, rounded side down, on ungreased baking sheets in a 425 °F (220 °C) oven, and bake for 10 minutes.*
**SMALL POTATO CUPS:** *Scrub, but do not peel, small potatoes. Cook them in boiling salted water for about 20 minutes, until tender. Drain and let cool. Cut them in half. Cut a very thin slice off the rounded end of each potato so that it stands upright. Hollow out each potato half with a melon baller or cut out a conical shape with a sharp paring knife.*
**LETTUCE LEAF SAUCERS:** *Wash the small inner leaves of lettuces, and dry them well.*

*Baby squash*

*Baby red pepper*

*Snow peas*

*Baby squash*

# MIDDLE EASTERN MEZZE

*Evoke the true spirit of hospitality with mezze — delicious snacks with which guests are welcomed at any time of the day throughout Greece and the Middle East. Mezze make ideal appetizers and party food, and offer an exciting range of flavors and textures.*

*Phyllo Pastries (pages 74–77)*
*and Dolmades (pages 78–79)*

*Middle Eastern*
*Meatballs (page 99)*

*Tomato & Zucchini
Cups (page 148) with
North African Style
Tuna Stuffing (page 24)*

*Apricot & Almond
Tartlets (page 118)*

*Hummus (page 30)
in pepper cups
with pita bread*

# DIPS FOR VEGETABLES

Aselection of dips served with raw vegetables or crudités arranged on a large platter makes an eye-catching item. Dips are ideal for serving at parties because they can be prepared up to a day in advance and kept tightly covered in the refrigerator. A number of the dips given here are spicy or piquant – perfect for pepping up subtle vegetable flavors. Choose your vegetable dippers from the suggestions given for the Aïoli Platter (see pages 32–33) and from the selection on page 149.

★

## MAYONNAISE

*I always make mayonnaise in a food processor because it's so incredibly quick and easy – and foolproof.*
*This recipe is for a basic mayonnaise, the most classic of dips. You can add chopped fresh herbs*
*just before serving if you like.*
*Makes 1½ cups (350 ml)*

### INGREDIENTS

*1 large egg*
*2 tsp red or white wine or sherry vinegar*
*1 tsp Dijon mustard*
*salt and freshly ground pepper*
*½ cup (125 ml) olive oil*
*1 cup (250 ml) canola or sunflower oil*
*1–2 tbsp lemon juice*

### PREPARATION

1 Put the egg, wine or sherry vinegar, mustard, and ½ tsp salt into the bowl of a food processor fitted with the metal blade. Process until all the ingredients are evenly combined.
2 With the food processor running, slowly add the olive oil a drop at a time, then add the other oil in a very thin stream, until it has all been absorbed. Add lemon juice and pepper to taste.

## ASIAN SESAME-GINGER DIP

*Makes 1 cup (250 ml)*

### INGREDIENTS

*¾ cup (175 ml) drained yogurt (see page 156)*
*¼ cup (60 ml) sesame oil*
*1 tbsp lemon or lime juice*
*1 tbsp rice vinegar*
*1 tbsp balsamic vinegar*
*1 small garlic clove, finely chopped or crushed*
*2 tsp finely chopped fresh ginger*
*2–3 tsp soy sauce*
*salt and freshly ground pepper*

### PREPARATION

Combine all the ingredients, adding soy sauce, salt, and pepper to taste.

## CREAMY CURRIED DIP

*Makes 1½ cups (350 ml)*

### INGREDIENTS

*¾ cup (175 ml) plain or nonfat yogurt*
*¾ cup (175 ml) mayonnaise*
*1½ tsp curry powder*
*½ tsp turmeric*
*½ tsp chili powder*
*¼ tsp ground ginger*
*¼ tsp paprika*
*salt and freshly ground pepper*

### PREPARATION

Combine all the ingredients, adding salt and pepper to taste.

## FRESH TOMATO SALSA

*Jalapeño peppers vary in intensity from mild to hot. Add sparingly and adjust the quantity by adding extra peppers after tasting the finished salsa.*
*Makes about 2½ cups (600 ml)*

### INGREDIENTS

*2 lb (1 kg) tomatoes, chopped*
*½ small red onion, finely chopped*
*1 tbsp red wine or balsamic vinegar*
*2–3 jalapeño or serrano peppers, cored, seeded, and finely chopped*
*4–5 tbsp chopped cilantro*
*salt and freshly ground pepper*

### PREPARATION

Combine all the ingredients, adding jalapeño peppers, cilantro, salt, and pepper to taste.

## TAHINI-YOGURT DIP

*Makes 1⅔ cups (400 ml)*

### INGREDIENTS

*1 cup (250 ml) plain nonfat yogurt*
*6 tbsp (90 ml) sesame tahini*
*¼ cup (60 ml) lemon juice*
*1–2 large garlic cloves, finely chopped or crushed*
*½ tsp ground cumin*
*salt and freshly ground pepper*

### PREPARATION

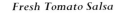

Whisk together all the ingredients with the garlic, cumin, and salt and pepper to taste. Adjust seasonings and thin out, if required, with water.

*Creamy Curried Dip*

*Fresh Tomato Salsa*

*Tahini-Yogurt Dip*

# Hummus

*Hummus, the Middle Eastern garbanzo bean purée, is delicious, easy to make, and can be prepared well in advance — in fact, it tastes better when made at least 1 day ahead. Serves about 10*

### INGREDIENTS

*2 large garlic cloves, peeled*
*1 1/4 cups (250 g) dried garbanzo beans, soaked, cooked, and drained (with some liquid reserved), or*
*15-oz (475-g) can garbanzo beans, drained (with some liquid reserved)*
*1/4 cup (60 ml) plain nonfat yogurt, more if needed*
*1/4 cup (60 ml) lemon juice*
*3 tbsp sesame tahini*
*2–3 tbsp olive oil*
*1/2 tsp ground cumin*
*salt*
*red and green peppers for serving (optional)*

### PREPARATION

**1** Turn on a food processor fitted with the metal blade, and drop in the garlic. When it is chopped, turn off the machine, and add the garbanzo beans. Process for about 30 seconds, until roughly chopped and grainy.

**2** Add half the yogurt with the lemon juice, tahini, 2 tbsp oil, cumin, and salt to taste, and process until smooth.

**3** From time to time, scrape down the side of the processor bowl. Thin out the hummus with some of the reserved bean liquid, or more yogurt or oil if preferred, to obtain a smooth consistency. Taste, and adjust seasonings.

**4** If serving hummus in pepper cups, cut off the stem ends of the peppers. Halve the peppers crosswise, and scoop out the cores and seeds. Fill with hummus and garnish as directed.

*Cooking tip: Garbanzo beans must always be soaked before cooking. Soak in water to cover by 2 in (5 cm) for at least 8 hours, or overnight.*

*If you are short of time, use the quick-soak method for cooking garbanzo beans: Place the garbanzo beans in a large saucepan and add enough water to cover by 1 in (2.5 cm). Bring to a boil, reduce the heat, and simmer for 2 minutes. Remove from the heat and let stand, tightly covered, for 1 hour.*

*Whichever method you use, discard the soaking water, and rinse and cook the beans in fresh water for 1 1/2–2 hours.*

# Baba Ghanouj

*This garlicky, lemony eggplant dip from the Middle East will have a deeper roasted flavor if you include some — or all — of the charred skin of the baked eggplant. Serves 10–12*

### INGREDIENTS

*2 lb (1 kg) eggplants*
*juice of 1 lemon, more to taste*
*2 garlic cloves, finely chopped or crushed*
*2 tbsp olive oil*
*2 tbsp plain nonfat yogurt*
*2 tbsp sesame tahini*
*1/4–1/2 tsp ground cumin*
*salt and freshly ground pepper*

### PREPARATION

**1** Cut the eggplants in half lengthwise, and score the cut sides with a sharp knife down to the skin, but not through it. Place the eggplant halves, cut side down, on an oiled baking sheet. Bake in a 450°F (230°C) oven for 20–30 minutes, until the skin is charred and shriveled. Remove from the heat and let cool.

**2** If you like the charred taste, leave the skin on the eggplants, otherwise remove it. Discard any seeds from the eggplants. Blend together the eggplants, lemon juice, garlic, oil, yogurt, tahini, and cumin to taste in a food processor fitted with the metal blade. Add salt and pepper to taste, and more lemon juice if you like.

# Bagna Cauda

*The Italian dip, Bagna Cauda, literally means "hot bath." Traditionally, it is served in an earthenware pot (see page 31), also called* bagna cauda, *which has its own small burner. You could use a fondue set or warming tray. Serves 4*

### INGREDIENTS

*1 small head of celery*
*1 cucumber*
*1 large red pepper*
*1/2 lb (250 g) baby eggplants*
*1 cup (250 ml) olive oil*
*3 tbsp (45 g) unsalted butter*
*3–5 large garlic cloves, finely chopped*
*8 anchovy fillets, rinsed thoroughly, patted dry, and chopped*
*salt (optional)*
*1/2 ciabatta loaf or peasant bread, sliced*

*Bagna cauda*

*Ciabatta slices*

**WARM DIP**
*Celery stalks, cucumber wedges, broiled red pepper strips and eggplant quarters, and sliced ciabatta bread accompany a Bagna Cauda.*

*Dipping vegetables*

## PREPARATION

**1** Wash the celery, and break it up into individual stalks. Cut the cucumber into long wedges. Core, seed, and cut the red pepper into 8 strips. Cut the eggplants lengthwise into quarters.

**2** Brush the red pepper strips and eggplant quarters with olive oil. Place under a medium-hot broiler for 3–5 minutes and cook, turning often, until lightly browned. Set them aside.

**3** Melt the butter in a heavy-bottomed saucepan over low heat. Add garlic to taste and cook until it softens. Do not let it brown at all.

**4** Stir in the anchovies, then slowly add the remaining olive oil in a thin stream, stirring and mashing the anchovies constantly with a wooden spoon. When all the oil has been added, the anchovies should have dissolved into a paste. Taste, and add salt if you like.

**5** Pour the dip into a bagna cauda or other flameproof pot set over a burner or candle. Serve immediately while the dip is still hot, with the vegetables and sliced ciabatta loaf for dipping.

# AïOLI PLATTER

This is a traditional Provençal dish consisting of a garlic-flavored mayonnaise dip with lightly cooked vegetables for dipping. I like to introduce other distinctively flavored dips to diversify the platter further. I usually steam or blanch the vegetables until just crisp-tender because they are easy to handle this way, but I also add a few uncooked red peppers and cherry tomatoes to add some bright, fresh color. There is sometimes fish on an aïoli platter. Here I have used shrimp; they are not traditional but they make the best finger food.

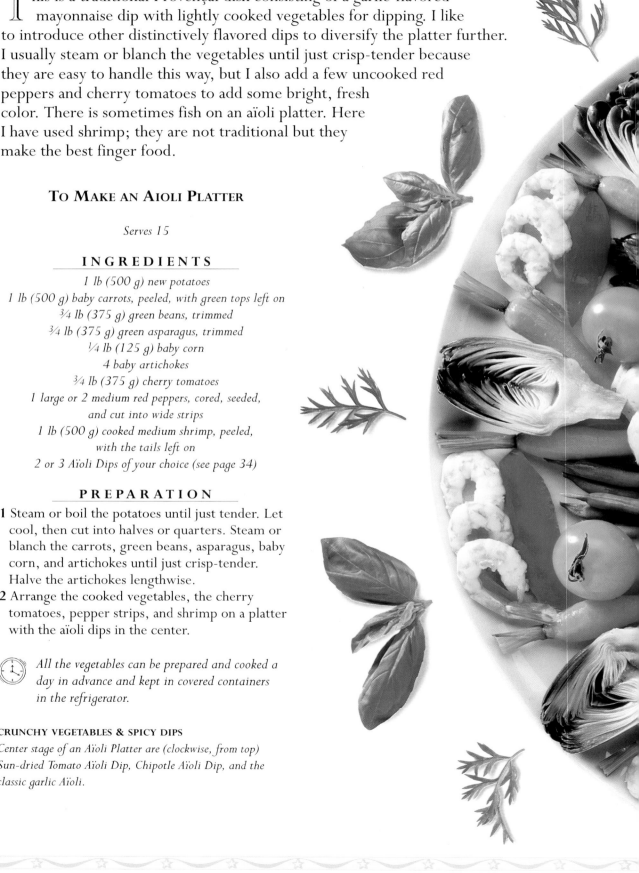

## TO MAKE AN AIOLI PLATTER

*Serves 15*

### INGREDIENTS

1 lb (500 g) new potatoes
1 lb (500 g) baby carrots, peeled, with green tops left on
¾ lb (375 g) green beans, trimmed
¾ lb (375 g) green asparagus, trimmed
¼ lb (125 g) baby corn
4 baby artichokes
¾ lb (375 g) cherry tomatoes
1 large or 2 medium red peppers, cored, seeded,
and cut into wide strips
1 lb (500 g) cooked medium shrimp, peeled,
with the tails left on
2 or 3 Aïoli Dips of your choice (see page 34)

### PREPARATION

**1** Steam or boil the potatoes until just tender. Let cool, then cut into halves or quarters. Steam or blanch the carrots, green beans, asparagus, baby corn, and artichokes until just crisp-tender. Halve the artichokes lengthwise.

**2** Arrange the cooked vegetables, the cherry tomatoes, pepper strips, and shrimp on a platter with the aïoli dips in the center.

 *All the vegetables can be prepared and cooked a day in advance and kept in covered containers in the refrigerator.*

**CRUNCHY VEGETABLES & SPICY DIPS**
*Center stage of an Aïoli Platter are (clockwise, from top) Sun-dried Tomato Aïoli Dip, Chipotle Aïoli Dip, and the classic garlic Aïoli.*

# AÏOLI DIPS

*Aïoli is a pungent garlic mayonnaise. Sun-dried tomatoes add extra flavor and a reddish hue,
while chipotle (smoked jalapeño peppers) add spiciness.
Make aïoli as mild or as strong as you like by varying the amount of garlic.*

★

## AÏOLI

*Aïoli will keep up to 1 day in the refrigerator but is best
made the day you wish to serve it.
Makes 1 1/2 cups (350 ml)*

### INGREDIENTS

*3–6 large garlic cloves, total weight 1/2–1 oz
(15–30 g), peeled and cut in half lengthwise,
green shoots removed
salt and freshly ground pepper
1 small potato, cooked, mashed, and strained (optional)
2 large egg yolks
1 1/2 cups (350 ml) olive oil
1 tbsp lemon juice (optional)*

### PREPARATION

**1** Pound the garlic using a mortar and pestle with
1/2 tsp salt until smooth. Mix in the prepared
mashed potato, if using.

**2** Beat the egg yolks at high speed in an electric
mixer fitted with a balloon whisk or egg
beaters, until smooth.

**3** Add the oil, a few drops at a time, and continue
to beat at high speed. Add half the oil in this
way, then add the remainder in a very slow,
thin stream, or 1 tbsp at a time. The mayonnaise
will be very thick. When all of the oil has been
added, mix in the garlic at low speed.

**4** Transfer to a bowl, taste, and stir in lemon
juice and pepper if you like.

### VARIATION

**INSTANT AÏOLI:** Stir the pounded garlic into
*1 1/2 cups (350 ml) bottled mayonnaise.* Omit the
potato and add *2 tbsp olive oil* for flavor.

—— *Food Processor Method* ——

*After completing step 1, break 1 whole egg instead of 2 egg
yolks into the bowl of a food processor fitted with the metal
blade. With the food processor running, slowly add the oil
in a very thin stream, or drop by drop. When all the oil has
been added, process in the crushed garlic.*

## SUN-DRIED TOMATO AÏOLI

*Makes 1 1/2 cups (350 ml)*

### INGREDIENTS

*3 large garlic cloves, peeled and cut in half lengthwise,
green shoots removed
salt and freshly ground pepper
1 small potato, cooked, mashed, and strained (optional)
2 large egg yolks
1 1/2 cups (350 ml) olive oil
1 tbsp lemon juice (optional)
4–5 oil-packed sun-dried tomatoes, rinsed and chopped*

### PREPARATION

**1** Pound the garlic using a mortar and pestle
with 1/2 tsp salt until smooth. Mix in the
prepared mashed potato, if using.

**2** Beat the egg yolks at high speed in an electric
mixer fitted with a balloon whisk or egg
beaters, until smooth.

**3** Add the oil, a few drops at a time, and continue
to beat at high speed. Add half the oil in this
way, then add the remainder in a very slow,
thin stream, or 1 tbsp at a time. The mayonnaise
will be very thick. When all the oil has been
added, mix in the garlic at low speed.

**4** Transfer to a bowl, taste, and stir in lemon
juice and pepper if you like.

**5** Transfer half the aïoli to another bowl and set
aside. Blend in the sun-dried tomatoes. Stir this
mixture into the plain aïoli.

### VARIATIONS

**CHIPOTLE AÏOLI:** Substitute *1–2 canned chipotle
chilis, drained, cored, seeded, and chopped*, for the
sun-dried tomatoes.

**LOW-FAT SUN-DRIED TOMATO OR CHIPOTLE
AÏOLI:** Substitute *3/4 cup (175 ml) low-fat fromage
blanc (see page 156) or plain nonfat yogurt* for half
the aïoli.

# EGGS & CHEESE

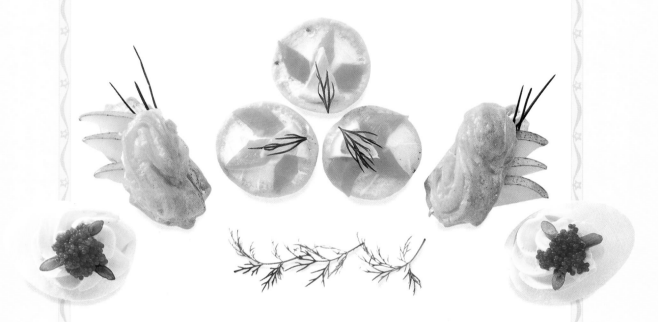

Here is a wide range of colorful frittatas,
spicy deviled eggs, elegant little blini, festive
gougères, and crêpes. You'll find the frittatas
incredibly easy to make, and they look so good. I love
making blini the focus of a party table, especially
when topped with smoked salmon and fromage blanc.
As I often have to prepare in advance for a party,
dishes such as frittatas, blini, and crêpes are ideal
because they can all be made long before.

# FRITTATAS

Almost every time I entertain, I make frittatas – flat Italian omelets. Cut into diamond shapes, they look beautiful on a party table. Make them a day ahead and keep them in the refrigerator, stacked in pairs. Cut them just before serving. You can add chopped fresh herbs, any type of vegetable, seafood, and meat to the basic frittata recipe below, or use the fillings on pages 38 and 39.

*Parsley*

## TO MAKE A FRITTATA

*Makes 60 x 1 1/2-in (3.5-cm) diamond shapes*

1 Beat together 10 large eggs and 3 tbsp milk with salt and freshly ground pepper to taste.

2 Prepare your choice of filling, and stir in.

3 Heat 1 tbsp olive oil in a 12-in (30-cm) nonstick skillet over medium-high heat. Pour in the egg mixture and stir with a fork.

4 Shake the pan gently, lifting up the edge of the frittata to let the egg mixture run underneath. Reduce the heat to low, cover, and cook for about 10 minutes. The eggs should be just set.

5 Brown the top of the frittata under a broiler for about 2 minutes. Let cool.

**BRIGHT & SAVORY DIAMONDS**
*Zucchini & Red Pepper Frittata (left and right on platter) flank Tender Pea & Pepper Frittata (above) and Smoked Salmon & Dill Frittata (below).*

*Black pepper*

*Salt*

*Zucchini*

*Red pepper*

## SERVING A FRITTATA

*Onion*

*1 Loosen the edge of the frittata from the pan with a spatula. Slide the frittata out of the pan.*

*2 Cut the frittata into diamond-shaped pieces, and arrange in a decorative pattern on a serving platter.*

Garlic

Milk

Beaten
egg

# FRITTATA FILLINGS

*Frittatas make an ideal base for any number of fillings. Depending on the ingredients used, they can encompass a wide range of flavors — the choice is all yours. Colorful and tasty ingredients are essential, so try to mix and match for best effect.*

★

## ZUCCHINI & RED PEPPER

*For a 12-in (30-cm) frittata*

### INGREDIENTS

*1–2 tbsp olive oil*
*1 large onion, chopped*
*1 large red pepper, cored, seeded, and diced*
*1 1/2 lb (750 g) zucchini, scrubbed and diced*
*2 large garlic cloves, finely chopped or crushed*
*salt and freshly ground pepper*
*3 tbsp chopped flat-leaf parsley,*
*or a mixture of parsley and other herbs,*
*such as basil, chives, tarragon, and chervil*

### PREPARATION

1 Heat 1 tbsp oil in a large, heavy-bottomed nonstick skillet over medium heat. Add the chopped onion, and cook for about 3 minutes, stirring often, until it begins to soften.
2 Add the red pepper, and cook, stirring, for a few minutes, until the pepper begins to soften.
3 Add the zucchini and garlic with salt and pepper to taste. Add 1 tbsp more oil, if necessary, or 2 tbsp water.
4 Cook for 5–10 minutes, stirring, until the zucchini is tender but still bright green.
5 Stir in the chopped herbs.

### VARIATION

**GREEN & RED PEPPER FRITTATA:** Substitute *2 large green peppers* for the zucchini and add *1 more red pepper*. For a sweeter taste, roast the peppers.

## SPINACH & FRESH HERB

*For a 12-in (30-cm) frittata*

### INGREDIENTS

*1 lb (500 g) spinach, stems removed, leaves washed*
*salt*
*leaves from 1 large bunch of flat-leaf parsley, chopped*
*1 cup (30 g) mixed fresh herbs, such as mint, chervil, chives, basil, and tarragon, chopped*
*2–3 large garlic cloves, finely chopped or crushed*

### PREPARATION

1 Blanch the spinach in a large pan of boiling salted water for 1–2 minutes, or put the spinach in a dry nonstick skillet with only the water left on the leaves after washing and toss over high heat for 1–2 minutes until wilted.
2 Rinse the spinach under cold water, squeeze dry in a dish towel, and chop.
3 Combine the spinach with the herbs and garlic.

## SMOKED SALMON & DILL

*For a 12-in (30-cm) frittata*

### INGREDIENTS

*1 tbsp olive oil*
*1 onion, chopped*
*3/4 lb (375 g) smoked salmon, diced*
*3 tbsp chopped fresh dill*

### PREPARATION

1 Heat the oil in a heavy-bottomed nonstick skillet over medium heat. Add the chopped onion, and cook about 5 minutes, stirring often, until tender.
2 Remove from the heat and stir in the diced salmon and dill.

*Smoked Salmon & Dill Frittata*

# GINGER, BEAN SPROUT, & CILANTRO

*For a 12-in (30-cm) frittata*

### INGREDIENTS

*1 tbsp canola or sunflower oil*
*2 bunches of scallions, both white and*
*green parts, thinly sliced*
*1 large red pepper, cored,*
*seeded, and diced*
*1/2-in (1-cm) piece of fresh ginger,*
*peeled and finely chopped or crushed*
*2 large garlic cloves, finely chopped or crushed*
*1 cup (250 g) bean sprouts, trimmed*
*and coarsely chopped*
*2–3 tsp soy sauce*
*2 cups (60 g) cilantro, chopped*
*salt and freshly ground pepper*

### PREPARATION

**1** Heat the oil in a large, heavy-bottomed nonstick skillet over medium heat. Add the scallions and red pepper, and cook for 1–2 minutes, stirring constantly, until the vegetables begin to soften.

**2** Add the ginger, garlic, and bean sprouts. Cook for about 1 minute, stirring.

**3** Drain off and discard any liquid which may have accumulated in the pan.

**4** Stir the soy sauce into the vegetables and remove the pan from the heat. Stir in the chopped cilantro.

**5** Taste, and adjust seasonings, adding more soy sauce or salt, and pepper to taste.

# ASPARAGUS

*For a 12-in (30-cm) frittata*

### INGREDIENTS

*1 lb (500 g) green asparagus, trimmed and cut*
*into 1/2-in (1-cm) lengths*
*3 tbsp chopped fresh chives*

### PREPARATION

Steam the asparagus for about 8 minutes, until tender and still bright green. Drain and rinse under cold water. Shake dry. Combine with the chopped chives.

# TENDER PEA & PEPPER

*For a 12-in (30-cm) frittata*

### INGREDIENTS

*1 tbsp olive oil*
*1 medium onion, chopped*
*1 large red pepper, cored, seeded, and diced*
*salt and freshly ground pepper*
*2 large garlic cloves, finely chopped or crushed*
*1 1/2 lb (750 g) fresh peas (unshelled weight), shelled,*
*or 3 cups (375 g) frozen peas*

### PREPARATION

**1** Heat the oil in a large, heavy-bottomed nonstick skillet over medium heat. Add the onion, and cook for about 3 minutes, stirring, until it begins to soften.

**2** Add the red pepper and a little salt, and stir together well. Cook, stirring often, until just tender, 5 minutes.

**3** Stir in the garlic, cook for 1 minute, then remove the mixture from the heat.

**4** If using fresh peas, steam them for 5–8 minutes, until tender, then rinse under cold water. Defrost frozen peas by dropping them into boiling water for 2 minutes, and then draining them.

**5** Stir the peas into the onion and pepper mixture, and add salt and pepper to taste.

---

## *FRITTATA FACTS*

- *Frittatas can be made in any sized skillet: the only requirement is that the pan should be heavy-bottomed in order to transmit and retain the heat and so produce an evenly cooked frittata. A nonstick coating also helps.*

- *Frittatas are cooked differently from omelets, which are cooked very quickly over high heat, whereas frittatas require slow cooking over low heat.*

- *While omelets should be moist and creamy, the perfect frittata is set and firm, without being dry.*

- *Omelets are served folded over, but a frittata takes on the shape of the pan in which it has been cooked.*

# DEVILED EGGS

Hard-boiled egg white halves make perfect containers for yolks speckled with freshly chopped herbs, enriched with tuna, or filled with pungent Provençal olives, capers, and anchovies. Mustard is used to pep up most of these fillings, although many other piquant flavorings are included. The eggs can be boiled and the fillings (minus lemon juice if among the ingredients) made a day ahead and refrigerated. Do not, however, fill and assemble the eggs more than an hour before serving or the fillings may discolor and separate.

**LITTLE DEVILS**

*Herb Potpourri filling is piped into hard-boiled egg halves and topped with salami and herb garnish (around platter). On the platter, Tapenade-filled egg coronets, garnished with parsley, are surrounded by eggs filled with piped Smoked Trout filling and garnished with smoked salmon diamonds and lemon zest.*

**Herb Potpourri
Deviled Eggs**

## To Make Deviled Eggs

*Makes 24*

**1** Put 12 large eggs in a saucepan with water to cover. Bring to a boil over medium-high heat, reduce the heat, and simmer for 10 minutes.

**2** Remove the eggs from the heat and run under cold water for several minutes until the eggs have cooled down.

**3** Peel the eggs and cut lengthwise in half, or, if you prefer, cut crosswise and shape into coronets as directed on page 43.

**4** Remove the yolks and use, where indicated, in the fillings given on pages 42–43.

**5** Pipe or spoon the fillings into the egg halves. Garnish if you like.

# DEVILED EGG FILLINGS

*Yolks from hard-boiled eggs combined with savory ingredients make delicious fillings for egg white halves. Eggs with well-centered yolks are easier to fill and look better.*

★

## HERB POTPOURRI

*Use any combination of fresh herbs for this green -and-yellow-speckled filling.*
*Add the lemon juice just before you fill the eggs — it will discolor the herbs if added too soon.*
*For 24 Deviled Eggs*

### INGREDIENTS

yolks from 12 hard-boiled eggs
$^1/_4$ cup (60 ml) nonfat yogurt
3 tbsp mayonnaise
2 tsp Dijon mustard
1–2 tbsp lemon juice
1 cup (30 g) finely chopped fresh herbs, such as parsley, tarragon, chervil, chives, thyme, dill, marjoram, and basil
salt and freshly ground pepper

### PREPARATION

1 In a food processor fitted with the metal blade, or using a mortar and pestle, blend the egg yolks, yogurt, mayonnaise, mustard, and lemon juice to taste until smooth (this can also be done by pressing the ingredients through a fine strainer).
2 Stir in the chopped mixed herbs, with salt and pepper to taste.

## SMOKED TROUT

*For 24 Deviled Eggs*

### INGREDIENTS

yolks from 6 hard-boiled eggs (reserve remaining 6 yolks for another use)
½ lb (250 g) smoked trout fillets
6 tbsp (90 ml) nonfat yogurt or fromage blanc (see page 156)
2 tbsp lemon juice, more if needed
2 tsp Dijon mustard
salt and freshly ground pepper

### PREPARATION

1 Combine the egg yolks with the trout in a food processor fitted with the metal blade.
2 Add the yogurt, lemon juice, and mustard to the trout mixture and process again until smooth. Add pepper to taste, then add more lemon juice and salt, if needed.

## CURRIED KEDGEREE

*Kedgeree, a smoked haddock rice dish invented during the British occupation of India, is traditionally garnished with hard-boiled eggs. In this recipe the roles have been reversed.*
*For 24 Deviled Eggs*

### INGREDIENTS

4 tbsp (60 g) butter
1 small onion, finely chopped
$^1/_2$ cup (125 g) long-grain rice
2 tsp mild curry paste or powder
$^1/_4$ tsp turmeric
1 cup (250 ml) milk and water mixed, for poaching
$^1/_2$ lb (250 g) smoked haddock fillets
2 tbsp plain yogurt or sour cream
yolks from 6 hard-boiled eggs (reserve remaining 6 yolks for another use)
1 tbsp chopped flat-leaf parsley
salt and freshly ground pepper
24 cooked, peeled shrimp, for the garnish
a little cayenne pepper, for the garnish

### PREPARATION

1 Melt the butter in a saucepan, add the onion, and sauté until soft. Add the rice and when it is transparent, add the curry paste or powder and turmeric. Add enough water to cover and simmer over low heat for about 20 minutes. The rice should be tender. Drain and let cool.
2 Bring the milk and water mixture to a boil, add the smoked haddock, and poach over low heat for 10 minutes. Remove and discard all the skin and bones from the smoked haddock and break up the flesh into very small pieces. Let cool.
3 In a large bowl, mix the curried rice, smoked haddock, yogurt, egg yolks, and parsley until well combined. Season the mixture with salt and pepper. Fill the egg whites and garnish each with a shrimp and a little cayenne pepper.

# TAPENADE

*Tapenade, the pungent Provençal paste, is incredibly versatile, serving not only as a unique filling for deviled eggs, but also as a topping for bruschetta and crostini, and as a stuffing for vegetables. It will keep 1 week in the refrigerator.*
*For 24 Deviled Eggs*

### INGREDIENTS

*2 large garlic cloves*
*1½ tbsp capers, drained and rinsed*
*4 anchovy fillets, rinsed*
*1 tsp fresh thyme leaves,*
*or ½ tsp dried thyme*
*1 tsp chopped fresh rosemary,*
*or ½ tsp crumbled dried rosemary*
*2 tbsp lemon juice*
*2 tbsp olive oil*
*1 tsp Dijon mustard*
*freshly ground black pepper*
*yolks from 6 hard-boiled eggs (reserve remaining*
*6 yolks for another use)*
*1⅓ cups (250 g) black olives, pitted and coarsely chopped*

### PREPARATION

1 Turn on a food processor fitted with the metal blade and drop in the garlic. When it is chopped, turn off the machine and add the capers, anchovies, thyme, and rosemary. Process until fairly smooth.
2 Add the lemon juice, olive oil, mustard, and black pepper to taste, and process again.
3 Add the egg yolks and process again until the mixture is smooth. Turn the mixture into a bowl and beat in the chopped olives.

---

### EGG SHAPES

• *For well-centered yolks, use only fresh eggs. The older an egg, the larger the air pocket inside. The yolk will travel toward this when the egg rests in the pan during boiling, resulting in a lopsided yolk cavity in the boiled egg.*

• *To make egg coronets, insert the tip of a small knife at an angle in the middle of the hard-boiled egg. Remove and reinsert in the opposite direction to meet the nearest tip of the first cut. Continue this zigzag pattern around the egg. Pull the serrated halves apart and remove the yolk.*

• *Once you have halved the eggs, cut a small slice off the base of each half so that it does not topple over.*

---

# CHICKEN, AVOCADO, & CORN

*This filling is made without the hard-boiled egg yolks.*
*For 24 Deviled Eggs*

### INGREDIENTS

*½ lb (250 g) cooked chicken, shredded*
*1 large avocado, peeled and finely diced*
*cooked kernels from 2 ears of corn*
*6 tbsp lime juice*
*1 large tomato, finely chopped*
*2 fresh hot green chilis, cored, seeded, and finely chopped*
*6 tbsp chopped cilantro*
*salt and freshly ground pepper*

### PREPARATION

Toss together all the filling ingredients, with salt and pepper to taste.

**Garnish suggestion:** *Reserve the hard-boiled yolks not used in this recipe to use here or elsewhere as a garnish. Press through a strainer, and sprinkle over the filled eggs or other party fare, such as Blini (see pages 46–47) or Nachos (see pages 82–83).*

# TUNA

*Tuna flavored with lemon juice makes a tangy and refreshing filling. This is a recipe you can put together from staples in your kitchen.*
*For 24 Deviled Eggs*

### INGREDIENTS

*2 x 6⅛-oz (173-g) cans water-packed tuna, drained*
*yolks from 12 hard-boiled eggs*
*2 tbsp olive oil*
*½ cup (125 ml) plain nonfat yogurt*
*1 tsp Dijon mustard*
*1–2 large garlic cloves, crushed*
*1–2 tbsp lemon juice, to taste*
*salt and freshly ground pepper*

### PREPARATION

1 Using a fork, flake the tuna until it is quite smooth. Add the egg yolks, olive oil, yogurt, and mustard, and mix together until fairly smooth.
2 Add the garlic and lemon juice, and salt and pepper to taste.

# BLINI WITH SAVORY TOPPINGS

These plump little pancakes are among my favorite party foods because they make marvelous vehicles for such a wide variety of toppings. From luxurious ingredients like smoked salmon and caviar to exotic tomatillo salsa and American style smoked turkey and mustard – you can be as creative as you like. A combination of dark buckwheat and light cornmeal blini provides an attractive contrast, both in color and flavor. You can make blini well in advance and freeze them: they can easily be heated from frozen and quickly assembled.

**BLOND BLINI**

*Cornmeal blini are an American variation on the traditional Russian buckwheat blini. They are an ideal base for piquant toppings such as Corn & Tomato Salsa and Cream Cheese & Radish Rose.*

*Corn & Tomato Salsa Blini*

*Cream Cheese & Radish Rose Blini*

**BROWN BLINI**

*Buckwheat blini make mouth-watering savory finger foods when topped with a range of fish and meats, such as Smoked Salmon & Fromage Blanc, Caviar & Fromage Blanc, and Smoked Turkey & Mustard.*

*Smoked Turkey & Mustard Blini*

*Smoked Salmon & Fromage Blanc Blini*

## TO MAKE TOPPED BLINI

*Makes 50*

**1** Make the blini as directed on page 146.

**2** To prevent the blini from becoming soggy, overlap rather than stack them on a plate when you transfer them from the pan. If you are not serving them immediately, the blini can be wrapped in a dish towel or foil. Reheat, wrapped in foil, in a 325°F (160°C) oven for 30 minutes.

**3** Prepare your choice of toppings from the recipes given on pages 46–47. Spoon, spread, or pipe onto the blini, and serve the blini as warm as possible.

*You can make blini in advance and freeze them. Stack them interleaved with waxed paper and wrap tightly in foil, then seal in a plastic bag. To defrost the blini, remove them from the plastic bag and heat the foil package in a 350°F (180°C) oven for 1 hour.*

*Caviar & Fromage Blanc Blini*

---

### INTERNATIONAL BLINI

*Blini are small, light pancakes made with yeast, and are part of the Russian tradition of zakuski, the ever-ready array of snacks and hors d'oeuvres. The batter for Russian blini is made from a mixture of buckwheat and white flours. Buckwheat is an easy grain to grow, because it does not require fertile soil. Originally, blini had a religious significance: they were eaten during the festivities of "butter week," the final days of the carnival that preceded and anticipated the abstinence and austerity of Lent. Today, wherever they are eaten, the Russian tradition*

*lingers on, because blini are typically served with caviar, smoked salmon or herring, and sour cream, usually as a snack for visitors, or as appetizers, with ice-cold vodka to complement their richness.*

*Cornmeal blini, an American invention, are lighter and more colorful than buckwheat blini, while French blini are made with white flour only. In France, blini can be bought ready made at charcuteries to accompany the smoked salmon that is usually sold there.*

# BLINI TOPPINGS

*A layer of fromage blanc, a sliver of smoked salmon, a wisp of dill, a few luxurious beads of caviar —
these are just a handful of the many delicious ingredients that make stunning toppings for blini.
You can follow my suggestions to the letter, or mix and match to create combinations of your own.*

★

## SMOKED TURKEY & MUSTARD

*This topping has only two ingredients. It is delicious served
on earthy-flavored buckwheat blini.
For 50 blini*

### INGREDIENTS

*1/2 lb (250 g) smoked turkey, thinly sliced
1/4 cup (60 ml) Dijon mustard*

### PREPARATION

**1** Cut the smoked turkey into 50 small diamond
or other shapes, using a small pastry cutter or
aspic cutter for a neat finish.

**2** Spread a little Dijon mustard thinly and evenly
on top of each blini and top with a piece of
smoked turkey.

## SMOKED SALMON
## & FROMAGE BLANC

*For 50 blini*

### INGREDIENTS

*about 2/3 cup (150 ml) fromage blanc or drained yogurt
(see page 156)
about 3/4 lb (375 g) smoked salmon, thinly sliced
freshly ground pepper*

### PREPARATION

**1** Spread about 1 heaping tsp fromage blanc or
yogurt on top of each blini.

**2** Cut the smoked salmon to fit the tops of the blini
and place on top of the fromage blanc or yogurt.
Sprinkle the salmon with pepper to taste.

## CAVIAR & FROMAGE BLANC

*Beluga caviar is superb on blini, but you can also use
salmon caviar. If you are using fine caviar, don't mix it
into the fromage blanc or yogurt mixture.
For 50 blini*

### INGREDIENTS

*1 1/2 cups (350 ml) fromage blanc or drained yogurt
(see page 156)
2 hard-boiled eggs, finely chopped
1 small red onion, finely chopped
2 oz (60 g) caviar
freshly ground pepper*

### PREPARATION

**1** Mix together the fromage blanc or yogurt, the
hard-boiled eggs, the onion, and, if using, the
salmon caviar. If using Beluga or other fine
caviar, omit the yogurt and fromage blanc and do
not mix in the caviar. Add pepper to taste.

**2** Top each blini with 1 heaping tsp of the mixture.
If using fine caviar, top each blini with the egg and
onion mixture, then place 1/2 tsp caviar on top.

---

### *GOLDEN EGGS*

*Caviar is matured sturgeon roe that has been salted to
preserve it. It is expensive because sturgeon is rare and the
female fish must be over 15 years old before the roe can be
made into caviar. Caviar comes chiefly from Russia and
Iran and is graded into three types, according to species,
color, and size:*

***Beluga,*** *the rarest and most expensive, comes from the
largest species of sturgeon. The eggs are large and very
fragile, and the color varies from pale to dark gray.*

***Osetra*** *is prized for its distinctive nutty flavor.
The rich golden brown eggs are smaller than Beluga.*

***Sevruga*** *is small and fine-grained and varies in color
from light to dark gray.*

# CORN & TOMATO SALSA

*This salsa is colorful and spicy, with contrasting textures as well as sweet and pungent flavors.*
*For 50 blini*

### INGREDIENTS

*kernels from 1 ear of corn*
*3 medium ripe tomatoes, finely chopped*
*1/2 small red onion, finely chopped*
*1–3 fresh hot green chilis, cored, seeded, and finely chopped*
*4 tbsp chopped cilantro*
*1 tbsp balsamic vinegar*
*salt*

### PREPARATION

1 Steam the corn kernels for about 5 minutes, until barely tender and quite juicy. Remove from the heat and rinse under cold water.
2 Mix together the tomatoes, onion, chilis to taste, cilantro, vinegar, and salt to taste.
3 Top each blini with the salsa, then with the corn, or mix the salsa and corn together if you like.

## Quick Blini Toppings

*To put together a few topped blini quickly, try these easy toppings:*

**CREAM CHEESE & RADISH ROSE:** Put *1 heaping tsp cream* cheese on each blini. Stuff *radish roses (see page 149)* with *cream cheese combined with diced tomatillo* and place on top. Garnish *with chopped chives.*

**RICOTTA CHEESE & RED PEPPER:** Chop or thinly slice *roasted red peppers,* then toss them with *finely chopped or crushed garlic* and *balsamic vinegar.* Put *about 1 tsp ricotta cheese* on each blini, then top with the pepper mixture and garnish with *fresh basil.*

# GREEN TOMATILLO SALSA

*For 50 blini*

### INGREDIENTS

*1/2 lb (250 g) tomatillos, husked, or 14-oz (425-g) can tomatillos, drained*
*2–3 fresh hot green chilis, cored and seeded*
*1/2 medium onion, roughly chopped*
*2 large garlic cloves, roughly chopped (optional)*
*6 sprigs of cilantro*
*salt*
*1/2 cup (125 ml) fromage blanc (see page 156), plain nonfat yogurt, or sour cream*

### PREPARATION

1 If using fresh tomatillos, cover in water in a pan and simmer for 10 minutes, then drain. Place fresh or canned tomatillos in a blender or a food processor fitted with the metal blade.
2 Add chilis to taste, the onion, garlic if using, and the cilantro sprigs. Process to a coarse purée. Transfer to a bowl and season with salt to taste. Let stand for 30 minutes or longer to allow the flavors to develop, before serving.
3 Top each blini with 1 tsp of the salsa, and about 1/2 tsp fromage blanc, yogurt, or sour cream.

# MANGO SALSA

*For 50 blini*

### INGREDIENTS

*1 ripe mango, peeled and finely chopped*
*2 small fresh green chilis, cored, seeded, and chopped*
*1 tbsp chopped cilantro*
*1/4 cup (60 ml) prepared Tomato Salsa (see page 29)*
*juice of 1 medium lime*

### PREPARATION

1 Toss together all the ingredients and let stand in a cool place for 1 hour.
2 Distribute the salsa evenly on top of the blini.

**Cream Cheese & Radish Rose Blini**

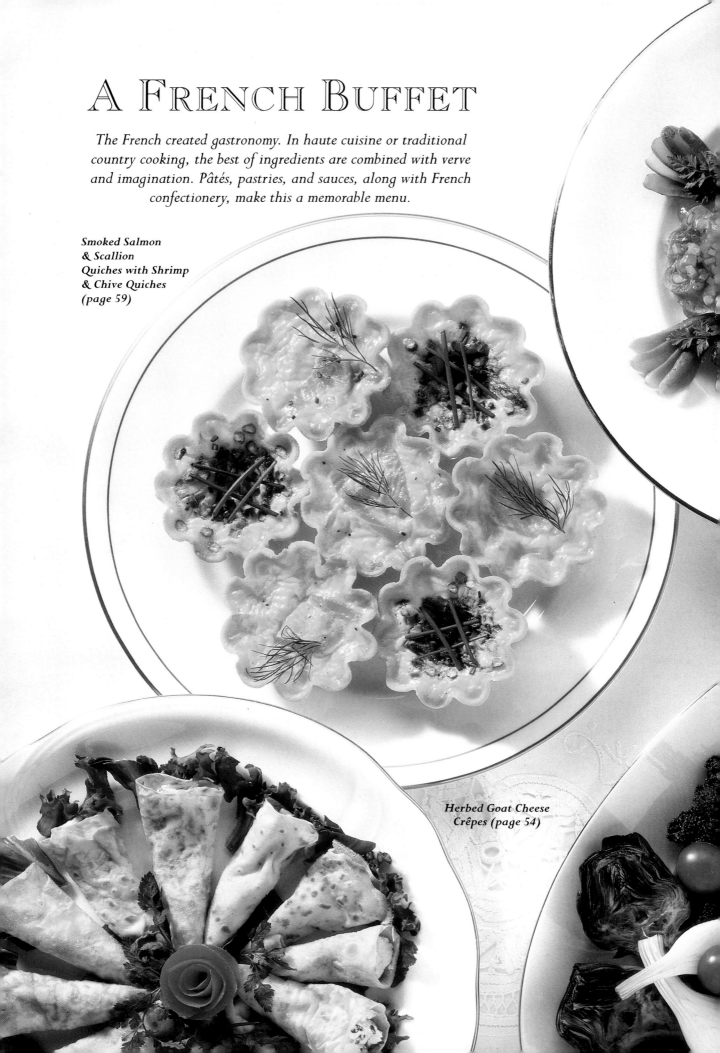

# A FRENCH BUFFET

*The French created gastronomy. In haute cuisine or traditional country cooking, the best of ingredients are combined with verve and imagination. Pâtés, pastries, and sauces, along with French confectionery, make this a memorable menu.*

**Smoked Salmon
& Scallion
Quiches with Shrimp
& Chive Quiches
(page 59)**

*Herbed Goat Cheese
Crêpes (page 54)*

Lamb Terrine en Gelée
(page 112) on canapés

Creamy Chocolate & Orange
Bouchées (page 125)

Aïoli Platter (page 32)

Lemon Sablés
(page 127)

# GOUGERES

Usually made in large rings, gougères are savory choux pastries. To serve as finger food, I make bite-sized pastries. Traditionally, they are made with Gruyère or Emmental cheese, so if you wish to keep with tradition, add ½ cup (60 g) grated cheese to the basic recipe on page 138.

★

## BLUE CHEESE & PEAR GOUGERES

*Makes 40*

### INGREDIENTS

½ cup (125 ml) nonfat fromage blanc (see page 156), or
6 tbsp nonfat cottage cheese and 2 tbsp plain nonfat yogurt
6 oz (175 g) blue cheese, roughly chopped
1 large ripe pear, peeled, cored, and finely chopped
¼ cup (30 g) blanched almonds, finely chopped
freshly ground pepper
40 bite-sized gougères (see page 138), baked and cooled

### PREPARATION

1 If using fromage blanc, blend together with the blue cheese in a food processor fitted with the metal blade, until smooth.
2 If using the cottage cheese and yogurt mixture, process them together first until smooth, then add the blue cheese and process again until smooth.
3 Stir in the chopped pear and almonds. Mix well and add pepper to taste.
4 Cut the tops off the gougères, and reserve for lids. Divide the filling evenly among the gougères, and replace the tops.

## GOAT CHEESE & PEPPER GOUGERES

*Makes 40*

### INGREDIENTS

2 red peppers
¾ lb (375 g) goat cheese
2 garlic cloves, roughly chopped
2–4 tbsp plain nonfat yogurt
salt and freshly ground pepper
40 bite-sized gougères (see page 138), baked and cooled

### PREPARATION

1 Grill the peppers until the skins are evenly charred, then seal in a plastic bag or place in a covered bowl until cool.
2 Skin, core, and seed the grilled peppers. Purée the flesh in a food processor fitted with the metal blade. Add the goat cheese and garlic and blend together. Add enough yogurt to thin out as desired. Add salt and pepper to taste.
3 Cut the tops off the gougères, and reserve for lids. Divide the filling evenly among the gougères, and replace the tops.

## CHICKEN PROVENÇAL GOUGERES

*This chicken filling tastes very good in cheese-flavored gougères. You can also use other light meats, such as poultry, pork, or veal, and blend them with robust Mediterranean ingredients to create strongly flavored, satisfying gougères.*
*Makes 40*

### INGREDIENTS

*½ lb (250 g) spinach, leaves washed, stems removed*
*salt and freshly ground pepper*
*2 cups (300 g) shredded cooked chicken, turkey, rabbit, pork, or veal, or a combination*
*2 tbsp olive oil*
*1 small onion, chopped*
*2 large garlic cloves, finely chopped or crushed*
*½ cup (125 ml) tomato sauce*
*½ cup (30 g) fresh bread crumbs*
*½ cup (15 g) finely chopped parsley leaves*
*2 tbsp chopped fresh rosemary*
*2 tsp fresh thyme leaves, or 1 tsp dried thyme*
*40 bite-sized gougères (see page 138), baked and cooled*

### PREPARATION

1 Blanch the spinach in a large pan of boiling salted water for 1–2 minutes. Alternatively, put the spinach in a dry nonstick skillet with only the water left on the leaves after washing. Toss over high heat for 1–2 minutes, until wilted.

2 Rinse the spinach under cold water, squeeze dry in a dish towel, and chop fine.

3 Finely chop the meat in a food processor. Add the spinach and mix together, using the pulse action of the food processor.

4 Heat the oil over medium heat in a heavy-bottomed nonstick skillet. Add the onion and cook, stirring, for about 5 minutes, until tender. Add the garlic and cook together for 1 minute. Remove from the heat.

5 Add the onion and garlic to the meat and spinach mixture with the sauce, breadcrumbs, and herbs, adding salt and pepper to taste. Mix together well.

6 Cut the tops off the gougères, and reserve for lids. Divide the filling evenly among the gougères, and replace the tops.

## MASHED POTATO & GARLIC GOUGERES

*The reason for blanching the garlic several times is to make it sweeter and less pungent.*
*Makes 40*

### INGREDIENTS

*2 large heads of garlic, cloves separated and peeled*
*3 quarts (3 liters) water*
*salt and freshly ground pepper*
*2 large potatoes, about 1 lb (500 g), peeled, cooked, mashed, and strained*
*2½ tbsp olive oil*
*40 bite-sized gougères (see page 138), baked and cooled*

### PREPARATION

1 Blanch the garlic: Put the cloves and 1 quart (1 liter) of the water in a saucepan and bring to a boil. Pour off the water. Add half the remaining water to the saucepan and bring to a boil. Pour off the water.

2 Add the remaining water and bring to a boil. Add 1 tsp salt, reduce the heat, and simmer for 30–40 minutes, until the garlic is very tender and the liquid fragrant. Remove from the heat.

3 Using a slotted spoon or skimmer, transfer the garlic from the broth to a food processor fitted with the metal blade. Process until thoroughly smooth.

4 Transfer to a large bowl and add the potatoes. Whisk or stir together until the mixture is well blended, then add the olive oil and 2 tbsp of the garlic broth. Add salt and pepper to taste.

5 Cut the tops off the gougères, and reserve for lids. Divide the filling evenly among the gougères, and replace the tops.

### Freezing Gougères

*Unfilled gougères freeze well. To defrost and crisp, place on a baking sheet, and heat through in a 425°F (220°C) oven for 4 minutes.*

# CREPES

Elegant little crêpe triangles stuffed with a variety of fillings make terrific finger food. Their great advantage is that the crêpes themselves can be made well in advance and stored in the refrigerator. Heat as directed below before filling and serving.

★

## MEXICAN STYLE FISH CREPES

*Makes 24*

### INGREDIENTS

12 peppercorns
1/4 tsp coriander seeds
1/4 tsp cinnamon or 1/4-in (5-mm) cinnamon stick
2 garlic cloves, peeled
1/2 tsp salt
2 tbsp water
2 tbsp canola or sunflower oil
1/2 small white onion, chopped
2 fresh green chilis, finely chopped
2 medium tomatoes, peeled and chopped
1 lb (500 g) fish fillets, such as shark,
mahimahi, or monkfish, cooked and shredded
12 crêpes (see page 147)

### PREPARATION

1 Grind the spices together. Pound the garlic using a mortar and pestle. Add the salt and ground spices. Grind together into a paste, then blend in the water. The mixture should be smooth.

2 Heat the oil in a heavy-bottomed saucepan or nonstick skillet over medium heat and add the onion. Cook, stirring, for about 3 minutes, until it begins to soften.

3 Add the chilis and tomatoes. Cook, stirring constantly, for about 5 minutes. Stir in the garlic and ground spice mixture. Continue to cook for 5 minutes.

4 Stir in the fish, mix well, and cook, stirring, 5 minutes. Remove from the heat, taste, and adjust seasonings.

5 Cut the crêpes in half. Warm them in a pan or in a 350°F (180°C) oven. Fill and fold the crêpes, as directed on page 53.

6 Arrange the crêpes on a serving platter, garnish as desired, and serve immediately.

## ASIAN STYLE CRAB CREPES

*Makes 24*

### INGREDIENTS

1/2 lb (250 g) cooked white crabmeat, shredded
5 scallions, both white and green parts, chopped
2 fresh hot green chilis
(or 1 green and 1 red), seeded, cored, and finely chopped
2 1/2 cups (75 g) chopped cilantro
1/4 cup (60 ml) canola or sunflower oil
2 tbsp dark sesame oil
1/4 cup (60 ml) lime juice
1 1/2 tsp soy sauce
2 tsp chopped or grated fresh ginger
1 large garlic clove, finely chopped or crushed
salt
12 crêpes (see page 147)

**FOR THE GARNISH (OPTIONAL)**
24 cooked, peeled shrimp
Tomato Rose (see page 154)
orange, lemon, and lime wedges
dill sprigs and basil leaves

### PREPARATION

1 Toss together the crabmeat, scallions, chilis, and cilantro.

2 Stir together the canola or sunflower and sesame oils with the lime juice, soy sauce, ginger, and garlic. Toss with the crabmeat mixture. Add salt to taste.

3 Cut the crêpes in half. Warm them in a pan or in a 350°F (180°C) oven. Fill and fold the crêpes, as directed on page 53.

4 Arrange the crêpes on a serving platter, garnish as illustrated, if you like, and serve immediately.

**CREPE FANTASY**

*Asian Style Crab
Crêpes are garnished with
shrimp, citrus wedges, herbs, and
a Tomato Rose (see page 154).*

## FILLING & FOLDING CREPES

*1 Place about 1 tbsp filling in the
center of each crêpe half. Spread it
evenly over one side of the crêpe.*

*2 Lift the unfilled side of the crêpe,
and fold it over the filling until the
two corners meet.*

*3 Fold the filled crêpe in half again,
to make a small triangular parcel,
with a little filling showing at the
open end.*

## HERBED GOAT CHEESE CREPES

*Makes 24*

### INGREDIENTS

*3/4 lb (375 g) goat cheese*
*6 tbsp (90 ml) plain nonfat yogurt*
*freshly ground pepper*
*2 tbsp chopped flat-leaf parsley*
*12 crêpes (see page 147)*

### PREPARATION

1 Put the goat cheese, yogurt, and pepper to taste in a bowl and mash them together well. Stir in the parsley.
2 Cut the crêpes in half. Warm them in a pan or in a 350°F (180°C) oven. Fill and fold the crêpes, as directed on page 53.
3 Arrange the crêpes on a serving platter, garnish as desired, and serve immediately.

## CHEESE & WILD MUSHROOM CREPES

*Makes 24*

### INGREDIENTS

*1 lb (500 g) wild mushrooms, such as cepes,*
*girolles, morels, or oyster mushrooms, stems trimmed,*
*thoroughly cleaned and dried,*
*sliced 1/4 in (5 mm) thick*
*salt and freshly ground pepper*
*1/2 cup (125 ml) dry, fruity red wine, such as*
*a Côtes du Luberon, a Gamay, or Beaujolais*
*1 tsp fresh thyme leaves, or 1/2 tsp dried thyme*
*1 tsp chopped fresh rosemary,*
*or 1/2 tsp dried rosemary, crushed*
*2 tbsp olive oil*
*2 large garlic cloves, finely chopped or crushed*
*2 tbsp chopped flat-leaf parsley*
*12 crêpes (see page 147)*
*1 cup (125 g) grated Gruyère cheese*

### PREPARATION

1 Cook the mushrooms and salt over medium heat in a nonstick skillet until they begin to release liquid. Cook, stirring, for 5 minutes or until the mushrooms just stick to the pan. Add the wine, thyme, and rosemary. Lower heat; simmer until wine is almost evaporated.
2 Add the olive oil, garlic, and pepper, and cook for about 5 minutes, stirring. Stir in the parsley and remove from the heat.

3 Cut the crêpes in half, sprinkle with grated Gruyère, and fill and fold as directed on page 53. Warm them in a 375°F (190°C) oven for 10–15 minutes, until the cheese melts.
4 Arrange the crêpes on a serving platter, garnish as desired, and serve immediately.

## PUMPKIN & ALMOND CREPES

*The filling for these crêpes is traditionally used for making Tuscan tortellini.*
*Makes 24*

### INGREDIENTS

*2 lb (1 kg) fresh pumpkin, seeds and membranes removed*
*3/4 cup (175 ml) fruity red wine, such as a*
*Beaujolais or Gamay*
*1/2 cup (60 g) almonds, peeled, toasted, and ground*
*1 cup (60 g) bread crumbs, preferably whole wheat*
*2 tbsp chopped fresh sage, or 1 tsp dried sage*
*2 tsp mild honey, such as clover or acacia*
*1/2 tsp ground cinnamon*
*1/4–1/2 tsp ground nutmeg*
*salt and freshly ground pepper*
*1/2 cup (60 g) freshly grated Parmesan cheese*
*12 crêpes (see page 147)*

1 Place the pumpkin in a lightly oiled baking dish, cover, and bake in a 400°F (200°C) oven for 45 minutes, or until tender. Remove from the oven and let cool.
2 Cut away the rind from the pumpkin. Pour off any juice from the dish, and purée the flesh in a food processor fitted with the metal blade.
3 Combine the wine, almonds, bread crumbs, sage, and honey in a large saucepan and heat until simmering. Stir together until the wine has been absorbed and no more liquid remains in the pan.
4 Stir in the pumpkin and cinnamon. Add nutmeg, salt, and pepper to taste. Remove from the heat and stir in the Parmesan.
5 Cut the crêpes in half. Warm them in a pan or in a 350°F (180°C) oven. Fill and fold the crêpes as directed on page 53.
6 Arrange the crêpes on a serving platter, garnish as desired, and serve immediately.

# QUICHES & SAVORY BREADS

*This chapter offers the widest range of finger foods
and appetizers. My passion for Italian and Provençal
food is apparent here — you'll find robust
Mediterranean flavors throughout in quiches, pizzas,
calzone, focaccia, bruschetta, and crostini. For the
most part, they are easy to make because quiches,
pizzas, and focaccia can be made in one large pan,
then cut into small pieces.*

# QUICHES

Small and crisp quiches baked with delicious and appealing fillings are always a great hit on a party table. I have given a choice of pastry doughs for making the quiche shells. The Pâte Brisée can be made either by hand or in a food processor, and can be made in advance and frozen, if you prefer. The Yeasted Olive Oil Pastry is very light and easy to make by hand.

*Asparagus Quiche*

### TO MAKE QUICHES

*Makes 8–10 x 3-in (7-cm) quiches*

**1** Choose your dough from the recipes given on pages 136–137.

**2** Once you have made the dough, line the pans. Unless you are freezing the pastry shells, you should refrigerate them for 2 hours.

**3** Prepare your choice of filling from the recipes given on pages 58–59.

**4** Bake the pastry shells blind in a 375°F (190°C) oven for 5 minutes.

**5** Fill the pastry shells with the filling of your choice, then bake for 20 minutes or longer (see recipe), until the tops are just beginning to brown and the fillings have set.

*Leek & Goat Cheese Quiche*

**SAVORY QUICHES**
*A tempting array of quiches offers a choice of fillings ranging from (around platter) Asparagus and Leek & Goat Cheese to (on platter) Smoked Salmon & Scallion; Spinach; Zucchini & Red Pepper; Wild Mushroom & Cheese; Shrimp & Chive; Herb & Scallion; and Cherry Tomato & Basil.*

*Asparagus Quiche*

---

### TO MAKE & SERVE A LARGE QUICHE

• *If you want to make one large quiche instead of 8–10 small quiches, the quantity of dough in each of the recipes given on pages 136–137 will make 1 x 10-in (25-cm) quiche. Each of the fillings given on pages 58–59 is enough for one large quiche.*

• *When you are ready to serve a large quiche, shape bite-sized portions in this simple and quick way: Cut the quiche into 1 1/2-in (3.5-cm) strips, then turn and cut the strips on the diagonal to make small diamond-shaped pieces. Serve the pieces from the quiche pan or arrange on a platter.*

*Leek & Goat Cheese Quiche*

*Asparagus Quiche*

# QUICHE FILLINGS

*I use fresh, light ingredients for quiche fillings. When baked, the egg and milk set into a custard to form a subtle base that highlights the contrasting flavors and textures of the other filling ingredients.*

★

## ASPARAGUS

*For 8–10 x 3-in (7-cm) quiches
or 1 x 10-in (25-cm) quiche*

### INGREDIENTS

*1 lb (500 g) green asparagus, trimmed
1 bunch of scallions, both white and green parts, chopped
1 tbsp olive oil or 1 tbsp (15g) butter
3/4 cup (90 g) grated Gruyère cheese
1/4 cup (30 g) freshly grated Parmesan cheese
4 eggs, beaten
3/4 cup (175 ml) milk
salt and freshly ground pepper
1 tsp fresh thyme leaves*

### PREPARATION

**1** Steam the asparagus for 5 minutes, until just tender. Refresh the asparagus in cold water and cut into 1/2-in (1-cm) lengths, reserving the tips for the garnish.

**2** Cook the scallions in the oil or butter, stirring, for 3–5 minutes, until tender. Mix with the asparagus and cheeses.

**3** Beat together the eggs and milk. Add 1/2 tsp salt, and pepper to taste. Combine with the asparagus and cheese mixture and the thyme leaves.

**4** Divide the filling among the shells and top with the asparagus tips.

### VARIATION

**SPINACH:** Substitute *2 1/2 lb (1.25 kg) fresh spinach* for the asparagus, and *1 chopped onion* and *2 finely chopped garlic cloves* for the scallions. Blanch the spinach in boiling salted water. Drain and refresh; drain again and cut into strips. Cook the onion and garlic in the oil, stirring, for about 5 minutes, until tender. Combine the spinach, onion, and garlic with the cheeses and *1 tbsp chopped fresh rosemary and thyme* and add to the egg and milk mixture with salt and pepper to taste.

## HERB & SCALLION

*For 6 x 4-in (10-cm) quiches or 1 x 10-in (25-cm) quiche*

### INGREDIENTS

*1/4 lb (125 g) scallions,
both white and green parts, chopped
1 tbsp olive oil
2 large garlic cloves, finely chopped or crushed
4 eggs, beaten
3/4 cup (175 ml) milk
salt and freshly ground pepper
3/4 cup (90 g) grated Gruyère cheese
1/4 cup (30 g) freshly grated Parmesan cheese
1 cup (60 g) chopped mixed fresh herbs, such as parsley,
tarragon, dill, thyme, marjoram, chives, and basil
(use at least 2 and not more than 4 types)*

### PREPARATION

**1** Cook the scallions in the oil, stirring, for 3–5 minutes until tender. Add the garlic and cook, stirring, for 1–2 minutes, until the garlic begins to color and smell fragrant.

**2** Beat together the eggs and milk. Add 1/2 tsp salt, and pepper to taste. Stir in the scallions and garlic, the cheeses, and chopped herbs. Mix together well.

### VARIATION

**ZUCCHINI & RED PEPPER:** Substitute *1 1/2 lb (750 g) zucchini, diced,* and *1 large red pepper, cored, seeded, and diced,* for the scallions. Substitute *3 tbsp chopped flat-leaf parsley* and *1 tsp fresh thyme leaves* or *1/2 tsp dried thyme* for the other herbs. Cook the diced pepper in the oil for about 3 minutes until it begins to soften. Add the zucchini, half the garlic, and salt to taste. Cook over medium-low heat, stirring often, for 10 minutes, or until the zucchini are tender but still bright green. If the vegetables begin to stick to the pan, add *1 tbsp water.* Add the remaining garlic, the herbs, and pepper to taste. Stir for about 1 minute, combine with the cheeses, and add to the egg and milk mixture.

## LEEK & GOAT CHEESE

*For 8–10 x 3-in (7-cm) quiches
or 1 x 10-in (25-cm) quiche*

### INGREDIENTS

*2¹/2 lb (1.25 kg) leeks, trimmed, white parts split in half
lengthwise, washed thoroughly, and thinly sliced
2 tbsp (30g) butter or 2 tbsp olive oil
1 tsp fresh thyme leaves, or ¹/2 tsp dried thyme
salt and freshly ground pepper
3 eggs, beaten
³/4 cup (175 ml) milk
³/4 cup (175 g) fresh goat cheese, crumbled
¹/4 cup (30 g) freshly grated Parmesan cheese*

### PREPARATION

1 Cook the leeks in the butter or oil, stirring
often, for about 10 minutes, until thoroughly
tender but not browned. Add the thyme and salt
and pepper to taste and remove from the heat.
2 Beat together the eggs, milk, and cheeses. Stir in
a little more salt and pepper. Combine this
mixture with the leeks.

## SMOKED SALMON & SCALLION

*For 8–10 x 3-in (7-cm) quiches
or 1 x 10-in (25-cm) quiche*

### INGREDIENTS

*1 bunch of scallions, both white and green parts, chopped
1 tbsp olive oil
4 eggs, beaten
³/4 cup (175 ml) milk
¹/4 lb (125 g) smoked salmon, diced
salt and freshly ground pepper*

### PREPARATION

1 Cook the scallions in the oil for about 5 minutes,
stirring, until tender.
2 Beat together the eggs and milk. Add the smoked
salmon, scallions, and salt and pepper to taste.
Stir well to mix.

### VARIATION

**SHRIMP & CHIVE:** Substitute *2 tbsp snipped chives*
for the scallions and *¹/2 lb (250 g) cooked, peeled
shrimp (thawed and drained if frozen)* for the
smoked salmon.

## CHERRY TOMATO & BASIL

*For 8–10 x 3-in (7-cm) quiches*

### INGREDIENTS

*4 eggs, beaten
³/4 cup (175 ml) milk
salt and freshly ground pepper
8–10 cherry tomatoes
1 small bunch of fresh basil, slivered*

### PREPARATION

1 Beat together the eggs and milk, with salt and
pepper to taste.
2 Put a cherry tomato in the center of each
quiche shell and slowly pour in the egg and milk
mixture. Sprinkle with the basil.

## WILD MUSHROOM & CHEESE

*For 8–10 x 3-in (7-cm) quiches
or 1 x 10-in (25-cm) quiche*

### INGREDIENTS

*2 medium shallots, finely chopped
1 tbsp olive oil
1 lb (500 g) fresh wild mushrooms,
cut into ¹/4-in (5-mm) thick slices
salt and freshly ground pepper
3 large garlic cloves, finely chopped or crushed
¹/2 cup (30 g) dried cepe mushrooms, soaked and drained
(see page 156), and coarsely chopped
¹/4 cup (60 ml) dry white or red wine
1 tbsp soy sauce
1 tbsp chopped fresh sage
1 tsp fresh thyme leaves, or ¹/2 tsp dried thyme
¹/2 cup (60 g) grated Gruyère cheese
¹/4 cup (30 g) freshly grated Parmesan cheese
4 eggs, beaten
³/4 cup (175 ml) milk*

### PREPARATION

1 Cook the shallots in the oil until tender. Add the
fresh mushrooms and a little salt. Cook, stirring,
until the mushrooms begin to release liquid, then
add the garlic and cepes. Cook for 2 minutes.
2 Add the wine, soy sauce, herbs, and pepper to
taste. Cook, stirring often, until all the liquid has
evaporated. Remove from the heat and place in
the shells.
3 Combine the cheeses and sprinkle over the
mushroom mixture. Beat together the eggs and
milk with salt and pepper to taste. Pour over
the mushroom mixture.

# CELEBRATING ITALY

Capture the essence of Italy in a sun-splashed array of dishes that
reflect the national colors of red, white, and green.
The delicious aromatic combination of
tomatoes, garlic, herbs, and olive oil is the
basis of most Italian finger food.

**Asparagus Frittata**
(page 39)

**Beef
Carpaccio**
(page 106)

*Clams on the Half Shell (page 102)*
*with Tomato Concassée (page 72)*
*and Basil Pesto (page 25)*

**Pizzettas with Herb & Garlic**
**with Parmesan topping**
**and Mozzarella & Tomato topping (page 64)**

*Coffee Macaroons (page 131)*

*Almond Biscotti (page 126)*

*Sun-dried Tomato Pizzetta*

*Cherry Tomato & Chive Pizzetta*

# PIZZAS & PIZZETTAS

Versatile is the best word to describe pizzas and pizzettas. I have provided a tempting selection of toppings, which can be made a day ahead and refrigerated. For fast ideas, go to Quick Toppings on page 70. Pizza dough can be refrigerated for a day or two, or frozen for several months. The dough can be made into large pizzas, then cut into diamond-shaped pieces after baking, or shaped into round, bite-sized pizzettas before baking.

*Anchovy & Caper Pizzetta*

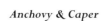

## TO MAKE PIZZAS & PIZZETTAS

*Makes 2 x 12–14-in (30–35-cm) pizzas or 16–20 pizzettas*

**1** Prepare the dough as directed on page 144.

**2** If the dough has not been rolled out before refrigerating or freezing, let it come to room temperature before rolling out your pizza or pizzetta bases. If you have already rolled out the dough, do not thaw it.

**3** Prepare your choice of topping from the recipes given on pages 64–65.

**4** Add your chosen topping to the pizza or pizzetta bases. In a 450°F (230°C) oven, bake pizzas for 20–25 minutes, and pizzettas for 15–20 minutes, until the crusts are crisp, browned, and fragrant. Serve hot or warm.

*Mozzarella & Tomato Pizzetta*

**A PIZZA PLATTER**
*A Sweet Pepper pizza cut into diamond-shaped pieces is encircled by pizzettas topped with (clockwise from top) Sun-dried Tomato, Cherry Tomato & Chive, Anchovy & Caper, Mozzarella & Tomato, and Olive & Parmesan.*

*Olive & Parmesan Pizzetta*

# PIZZA & PIZZETTA TOPPINGS

*Ingredients such as sweet and wonderful red and yellow peppers cooked slowly in olive oil, luscious wild mushrooms, ripe tomatoes, and fragrant herbs make mouth-watering toppings for pizzas.*

★

## TOMATO & PESTO

*For 2 x 12–14-in (30–35-cm) pizzas or 16–20 pizzettas*

### INGREDIENTS

*3–4 large garlic cloves, finely chopped or crushed*
*1 tbsp olive oil*
*3 lb (1.5 kg) canned or fresh tomatoes,*
*peeled, seeded, and chopped*
*1/4 tsp sugar*
*salt and freshly ground pepper*
*1 tsp dried oregano or thyme, or 2 tbsp slivered fresh basil*
*about 3/4 cup (175 ml) Basil Pesto (see page 25)*
*1/2 cup (60 g) freshly grated Parmesan cheese*

### PREPARATION

**1** Cook the garlic in the oil. When it begins to color, add the tomatoes, sugar, salt to taste, and the dried herbs, if using. Cook, stirring often, for 20–30 minutes, until the tomatoes are reduced.

**2** Stir in the basil, if using, and cook over low heat for 1–2 minutes. Add pepper to taste and remove from the heat.

**3** Pour into a food processor fitted with the metal blade and process for about 30 seconds. Taste, and adjust seasonings.

**4** Spoon the tomato sauce over the pizza or pizzetta bases. Add 1 tsp pesto to each pizzetta base, or divide the pesto between each large pizza. Sprinkle with the grated Parmesan.

### VARIATIONS

**SUN-DRIED TOMATO:** Substitute *sliced sun-dried tomatoes* for the pesto, and *1/2 tsp dried oregano* for the Parmesan.

**CHERRY TOMATO & CHIVE:** Substitute *sliced cherry tomatoes* for the pesto, and top the Parmesan with *fresh chives*.

**MOZZARELLA & TOMATO:** Substitute *cubes of mozzarella cheese* for the pesto and Parmesan, and sprinkle with *chopped fresh herbs*.

**OLIVE & PARMESAN:** Substitute *rings of sliced pitted black olives* for the pesto; sprinkle the Parmesan in the center.

**ANCHOVY & CAPER:** Substitute *16 canned anchovy fillets* for the pesto, and *4 tbsp capers* for the Parmesan.

## TOMATO & CAPER

*For 2 x 12–14-in (30–35-cm) pizzas or 16–20 pizzettas*

### INGREDIENTS

*3 tbsp olive oil*
*1/2 cup (60 g) freshly grated Parmesan cheese*
*8 large garlic cloves, 6 thinly sliced*
*and 2 finely chopped or crushed*
*2 lb (1 kg) plum tomatoes, peeled,*
*juice and seeds squeezed out, and chopped*
*2 tsp dried oregano or 2 tbsp chopped fresh basil*
*salt and freshly ground pepper*
*4 tbsp capers, drained and rinsed*
*black olives (optional)*
*4 artichoke hearts, drained and sliced (optional)*
*12 anchovy fillets, rinsed and cut in half (optional)*

### PREPARATION

**1** Brush the pizza or pizzetta bases with half the olive oil and sprinkle with half the Parmesan. Scatter the sliced garlic over the Parmesan.

**2** Toss together the tomatoes, the chopped garlic, the oregano or basil, and salt and pepper to taste. Spoon over the sliced garlic and top with the capers, any of the optional ingredients, and the remaining Parmesan. Drizzle over the remaining olive oil.

## HERB & GARLIC WITH PARMESAN

*For 2 x 12–14-in (30–35-cm) pizzas or 16–20 pizzettas*

### INGREDIENTS

*3 tbsp olive oil*
*3–4 garlic cloves, finely chopped or crushed*
*4 tbsp chopped fresh rosemary, sage, or oregano, or a mixture*
*1/4 cup (30 g) freshly grated Parmesan cheese*

### PREPARATION

**1** Mix together the oil and garlic. Brush each pizza or pizzetta base generously with this mixture.

**2** Sprinkle the chopped herbs over the oil and garlic mixture. Top with the Parmesan.

## SWEET PEPPER

*For 2 x 12–14-in (30–35-cm) pizzas or 16–20 pizzettas*

### INGREDIENTS

*2 medium onions, unpeeled (optional)*
*6 large peppers (red and/or yellow), cored, seeded, and cut into long thin strips*
*3 tbsp olive oil*
*coarse sea salt and freshly ground pepper*
*3 large garlic cloves, finely chopped or crushed*
*2 tbsp slivered fresh basil*
*2 tsp fresh thyme leaves*
*1 lb (500 g) tomatoes, peeled, seeded, and chopped*

### PREPARATION

**1** If using the onions, bake them for 1¼ hours in a 400°F (200°C) oven, turning them every 15 minutes. Remove from the oven and let cool.
**2** Peel off and discard the burnt outer layers of the onions. Cut the onions into long thin slices.
**3** Cook the pepper strips in 1 tbsp of the oil, until they begin to sizzle. Sprinkle with salt and pepper, reduce the heat, cover, and cook for 15 minutes, stirring often, until tender.
**4** Stir in two-thirds of the garlic, the basil, and thyme and remove from the heat. Taste, and adjust seasonings.
**5** Toss the chopped tomatoes with the remaining garlic and salt and pepper to taste. Layer the tomatoes, peppers, and onions over the pizza or pizzetta bases. Drizzle over the remaining oil.

## PROVENÇAL ONION

*For 2 x 12–14-in (30–35-cm) pizzas or 16–20 pizzettas*

### INGREDIENTS

*4 lb (2 kg) white or yellow onions, finely chopped*
*coarse sea salt and freshly ground pepper*
*5–6 tbsp (75–90 ml) olive oil*
*4 garlic cloves, finely chopped or crushed*
*3–4 tsp fresh thyme leaves, or 1–2 tsp dried thyme*
*2 tbsp capers, drained, rinsed, and crushed*
*32 anchovy fillets, rinsed and cut in half*
*16–20 Niçoise olives*

### PREPARATION

**1** Cook the onions, with about ½ tsp sea salt, in the oil. When the onions begin to sizzle, add the garlic, thyme, and pepper to taste.
**2** Reduce the heat, cover, and cook slowly for about 45 minutes, stirring often, until the onions have melted to a purée. Stir in the capers, then taste, and adjust seasonings. Spread over pizza or pizzetta bases. Top with the anchovies and olives.

## WILD MUSHROOM & HERB

*For 2 x 12–14-in (30–35-cm) pizzas or 16–20 pizzettas*

### INGREDIENTS

*2 medium shallots, finely chopped*
*3 tbsp olive oil*
*1 lb (500 g) fresh wild mushrooms, trimmed, rinsed, and cut into ¼-in (5-mm) slices*
*salt and freshly ground pepper*
*3 large garlic cloves, finely chopped or crushed*
*½ cup (30 g) dried cepe mushrooms, soaked and drained (see page 156), and coarsely chopped*
*¼ cup (60 ml) dry white or red wine*
*1 tbsp soy sauce*
*1 tbsp chopped fresh sage, or 2 tsp chopped fresh rosemary*
*1 tsp fresh thyme leaves, or ½ tsp dried thyme*

### PREPARATION

**1** Cook the shallots in 1 tbsp of the oil, stirring, until tender and beginning to brown. Add the fresh mushrooms and a little salt. Cook, stirring, until the mushrooms begin to release water.
**2** Add the garlic and cepes and cook, stirring, for 2 minutes. Add the wine, soy sauce, herbs, and pepper to taste. Continue to cook until the liquid has just about evaporated and the mushrooms are tender.
**3** Spread the mixture over the pizza or pizzetta bases. Drizzle over the remaining oil.

# CALZONE & FOCACCIA

*Calzone and focaccia are variations of pizzas. Calzone are pizzas folded to make turnovers shaped like half-moons. Focaccia is a flat bread like a thick pizza. For parties, I make bite-sized calzone and cut focaccia into small squares.*

★

## GOAT CHEESE & HERB CALZONE

*Makes 36*

### INGREDIENTS

1 recipe risen pizza dough (see page 144)
1 lb (500 g) mild fresh goat cheese
3 tbsp plain nonfat yogurt
1/2 cup (60 g) freshly grated Parmesan cheese
2 garlic cloves, finely chopped or crushed
1/2 cup (30 g) fresh herbs, such as parsley, basil, thyme, rosemary, sage, and oregano, chopped
2 tbsp chopped fresh chives
salt and freshly ground pepper
1/4 cup (60 ml) olive oil, mixed with
2 garlic cloves, finely chopped or crushed (optional)

### PREPARATION

**1** Make pizza dough as directed on page 144, up to the end of step 4. Punch down the dough and divide it into 3 equal pieces. Divide each of these into 6 pieces, then cut each of the 6 pieces in half, to form 36 pieces in all. Form small balls with the pieces, and cover. Let rest for 15 minutes.

**2** Mix together the goat cheese and yogurt. Stir in the Parmesan, garlic, mixed herbs, and chives. Add salt and pepper to taste.

**3** Roll out each ball of dough into an oval shape, about 1/8–1/4 in (3–5 mm) thick. Brush with garlic-flavored oil, if using.

**4** Place 2 tsp of the filling on one half of each calzone oval. Fold the top half of the calzone over to meet the bottom edge, making a half-moon shape. Pinch the edges together, then fold the edge in once and twist it to make an attractive lip.

**5** Make one or two small slits in the top of each calzone to allow the steam to escape during baking and prevent the calzone from bursting.

**6** Bake the calzone on lightly oiled, cornmeal- or semolina-dusted baking sheets, in a 450°F (230°C) oven for 15–20 minutes, or until the calzone are brown and crisp around the edges.

## TOMATO & BASIL CALZONE

*Makes 36*

### INGREDIENTS

1 recipe risen pizza dough (see page 144)
2 garlic cloves, finely chopped or crushed
1 tbsp olive oil
3 lb (1.5 kg) canned or fresh tomatoes, peeled, seeded, and chopped
1/4 tsp sugar
salt and freshly ground pepper
3 tbsp slivered fresh basil
3 oz (90 g) mozzarella cheese, cut into 36 pieces
3 tbsp freshly grated Parmesan cheese

### PREPARATION

**1** Make pizza dough as directed on page 144, up to the end of step 4. Punch down the dough and divide it into 3 equal pieces. Divide each of these into 6 pieces, then cut each of the 6 pieces in half, to form 36 pieces in all. Form small balls with the pieces, and cover. Let rest for 15 minutes.

**2** Cook the garlic in the olive oil. Add the tomatoes with the sugar, and salt to taste. Cook, stirring often, until the tomatoes are reduced. Remove from the heat.

**3** Stir in the basil, and pepper to taste.

**4** Roll out each ball of dough into an oval shape, about 1/8–1/4 in (3–5 mm) thick.

**5** Place 1 heaping tsp tomato sauce on one half of each calzone oval, top with a piece of mozzarella and a pinch of grated Parmesan. Fold the top half of the calzone over to meet the bottom edge, making a half-moon shape. Pinch the edges together, then fold the edge in once, and twist it to make an attractive lip.

**6** Make one or two small slits in the top of each calzone to allow the steam to escape during baking and prevent the calzone from bursting.

**7** Bake the calzone on lightly oiled, cornmeal- or semolina-dusted baking sheets, in a 450°F (230°C) oven for 15–20 minutes, or until the calzone are brown and crisp around the edges.

# MUSHROOM & RICOTTA CALZONE

*Makes 36*

### INGREDIENTS

*1 recipe risen pizza dough (see page 144)*
*1 garlic clove, finely chopped or crushed*
*1 tbsp olive oil*
*1 cup (60 g) dried cepe mushrooms, soaked and drained (see page 156), and coarsely chopped*
*2 tbsp dry white wine*
*2 tsp chopped fresh rosemary*
*1 tsp fresh thyme leaves*
*salt and freshly ground pepper*
*3/4 lb (375 g) low-fat ricotta cheese*
*3/4 cup (90 g) freshly grated Parmesan cheese*

### PREPARATION

**1** Make pizza dough as directed on page 144, up to the end of step 4. Punch down the dough and divide it into 3 equal pieces. Divide each of these into 6 pieces, then cut each of the 6 pieces in half, to form 36 pieces. Form small balls with the pieces, and cover. Let rest for 15 minutes.
**2** Cook the garlic in the oil until it begins to color. Add the cepes and stir for 1 minute. Add the wine, herbs, and salt and pepper to taste, and stir until the wine evaporates; remove from the heat.
**3** Mix the two cheeses into the mushroom mixture.
**4** Roll out each ball of dough into an oval shape, about 1/8–1/4 in (3–5 mm) thick.
**5** Place 2 tsp of the filling on one half of each calzone oval. Fold the top half of the calzone over to meet the bottom edge, making a half-moon shape. Pinch the edges together, then fold the edge in once, and twist it to make an attractive lip.
**6** Make one or two small slits in the top of each calzone to allow the steam to escape during baking and prevent the calzone from bursting.
**7** Bake the calzone on lightly oiled, cornmeal- or semolina-dusted baking sheets, in a 450°F (230°C) oven for 15–20 minutes, or until the calzone are brown and crisp around the edges.

---

### ITALIAN FAST FOOD

*Focaccia is the traditional pizza base. In Italy it is also served as a savory bread, often garnished with herbs, or it is slit, filled with cold cuts, such as salami, and cut into pieces to form sandwiches.*

---

# SAGE & ONION FOCACCIA

*Makes 35 x 2-in (5-cm) squares*

### INGREDIENTS

*1 recipe focaccia dough (see page 145)*
*5 tbsp (75 ml) olive oil*
*1 1/2 lb (750 g) onions, chopped*
*1/2 tsp coarse sea salt*
*30 fresh sage leaves, chopped, more for garnish*

### PREPARATION

**1** Make focaccia dough as directed on page 145, up to the end of step 4.
**2** While the dough is rising, heat 2 tbsp of the oil in a heavy-bottomed nonstick skillet over medium heat. Add the onions and salt. Cook, stirring, for 15 minutes, until the onions are tender and beginning to brown.
**3** Remove the onions from the heat and stir in the chopped sage. Let cool.
**4** Knead the dough and shape into 2 balls as directed in step 5 on page 145 and continue until the end of step 6. Brush the focaccia with olive oil and spread the onion and sage mixture over the tops. Cover, and let rise for 1 hour.
**5** Bake in a 400°F (200°C) oven, preferably with a baking stone (see page 156), for 20–25 minutes.
**6** Cool on racks, then cut into 2-in (5-cm) squares and garnish with small sage leaves.

# OLIVE FOCACCIA

*Makes 35 x 2-in (5-cm) squares*

### INGREDIENTS

*1 recipe focaccia dough (see page 145)*
*1 1/2 cups (225 g) black olives, pitted and chopped, more for garnish (optional)*
*1 tbsp olive oil*

### PREPARATION

**1** Make focaccia dough as directed on page 145, up to the end of step 3, but do not shape into a ball.
**2** Add the olives to the focaccia dough, and knead again to incorporate them evenly.
**3** Shape the dough into a ball, and proceed from step 4 in the basic recipe on page 145. If you like, garnish the focaccia with black olives set in the dimples before baking.
**4** Cut into 2-in (5-cm) squares.

# RUSTIC ITALIAN BRUSCHETTA & CROSTINI

Thank goodness the boring canapés of yesteryear have given way to today's gutsy Mediterranean inspired bruschetta and crostini. Bruschetta are crisp on the outside but still bready in the center, while thinner crostini are more like croutons. Bruschetta and crostini can only be as good as the bread from which they are made. I like to make my own sourdough or herbed bread, but for a large buffet party I buy the best hard-crusted country bread or herb bread available for bruschetta, and baguettes to make crostini.

**CROSTINI**
*Crouton-like crostini make crisp bases for any number of Italian style toppings, including Tomato & Mozzarella.*

*Tomato & Mozzarella Crostini*

**Anchovy Bruschetta**

**BRUSCHETTA**
*Unpretentious canapés, bruschetta conceal a soft interior within thick, crusty slices. Piquant toppings, such as Anchovy, garnished with capers and scallions, and Roast Pepper & Mozzarella, with sliced pepperoni and flaked tuna, add to their rustic appeal.*

*Roast Pepper & Mozzarella Bruschetta*

## To Make Bruschetta & Crostini

*Makes 18–24 bruschetta or crostini*

**1 For Bruschetta,** cut 1 loaf of crusty bread into 9–12 slices ¾-in (2-cm) thick.

**2** Set under a preheated broiler, about 4–5 in (10–12 cm) from the heat, and toast for 1 minute, or less, per side – the bread should remain soft inside.

**3** Remove the toasted slices of bread from the heat and immediately rub them vigorously with 1–2 large garlic cloves, sliced in half lengthwise. Brush with 2–3 tbsp olive oil. Cut the slices in half. Keep the bruschetta warm in a low oven.

**4** Top with your chosen topping and heat through (see recipes on pages 70–71).

**1 For Crostini,** cut 1 large baguette into 9–12 slices ½-in (1-cm) thick.

**2** Set under a preheated broiler, about 4–5 in (10–12 cm) from the heat, and toast until lightly browned on both sides.

**3** If serving the same day, rub the bread with 1–2 large garlic cloves, sliced in half lengthwise, then brush with 2–3 tbsp olive oil. If making in advance, let cool, then keep in an airtight container for up to 2 days. Rub with garlic and brush with olive oil before topping and serving.

**4** Top with your chosen topping and heat through (see recipes on pages 70–71).

*Tomato & Mozzarella Crostini*

*Anchovy Bruschetta*

*Roast Pepper & Mozzarella Bruschetta*

# BRUSCHETTA & CROSTINI TOPPINGS

*Add any of these luscious toppings to garlic-scented toasted bread to create memorable bite-sized appetizers. Robust flavors from typical Mediterranean ingredients, such as peppers and tomatoes, anchovies and capers, add to the pleasure of biting into the crunchy bases.*

★

## ROAST PEPPER & MOZZARELLA

*For 18–24 bruschetta or 36–48 crostini*

### INGREDIENTS

2 lb (1 kg) red peppers, or a combination of red and yellow peppers
2 large garlic cloves, finely chopped or crushed
2 tbsp olive oil
2 tbsp slivered fresh basil leaves
coarse sea salt and freshly ground pepper
¼ lb (125 g) fresh or smoked mozzarella cheese, cut into thin slivers

### PREPARATION

1 Bake the peppers in a 400°F (200°C) oven for 30–45 minutes, turning every 10 minutes, until the peppers are soft and the skin is puffed and brown in places.

2 Carefully transfer the peppers to a bowl. Cover tightly with a plate and let the peppers cool for 20–30 minutes, by which time they will have softened and released plenty of liquid. Reduce the oven temperature to 375°F (190°C).

3 Peel, core, and halve the peppers while holding them over a bowl to catch the juices, then remove the seeds and white ribs. Slice into thin strips and place in another bowl.

4 Strain all the liquid from the peppers over the slices in the bowl. Toss with the garlic, olive oil, basil, and salt and pepper to taste. Marinate for at least 30 minutes.

5 Place a sliver of mozzarella on each bruschetta and top with the pepper mixture. Bake in the oven for 5–10 minutes, until the cheese begins to melt. Serve hot.

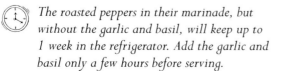 *The roasted peppers in their marinade, but without the garlic and basil, will keep up to 1 week in the refrigerator. Add the garlic and basil only a few hours before serving.*

---

### Quick Toppings

*There are many ingredients, such as ready-made bottled sauces and dips, that can be used to make delicious toppings for bruschetta and crostini in a matter of minutes. Here are just a few of my suggestions:*

**PESTO:** *Pesto with cooked scallops and cooked, peeled shrimp, garnished with fresh basil or chervil.*

**SALSA:** *Salsa with cooked scallops, cooked, peeled shrimp, chopped smoked turkey, or smoked trout, garnished with fresh cilantro.*

**FROMAGE BLANC:** *Fromage blanc (see page 156), crème fraîche, or ricotta, with caviar spooned in the center.*

**HUMMUS:** *Hummus sprinkled with fresh parsley or garnished with thin lemon slices.*

**TARAMASALATA:** *Taramasalata garnished with salmon roe.*

**RICOTTA:** *Ricotta cheese with slivered sun-dried tomatoes or sliced Italian or French dried sausage.*

**PATE:** *Any meat, fish, or vegetable pâté sprinkled with chopped fresh herbs.*

**CANNED WHITE BEAN:** *Canned white or garbanzo beans, mashed and seasoned with lemon juice, olive oil, and garlic, sprinkled with chopped fresh herbs, or topped with sliced dried sausage or smoked ham.*

**FRESH HERB:** *Fresh herbs, such as tarragon, basil, dill, chervil, and parsley, washed and chopped.*

**SMOKED MACKEREL:** *Canned smoked mackerel, drained and flaked, topped with thin slices of lemon.*

**SMOKED SALMON:** *Thin slices of smoked salmon topped with capers.*

**TOMATO & OLIVE:** *Bottled tomato sauce garnished with pitted black olives.*

**ARUGULA & PARMESAN:** *Chopped arugula leaves garnished with thin slivers of Parmesan cheese.*

## ANCHOVY

*For 18–24 bruschetta or 36–48 crostini*

### INGREDIENTS

*1–2 garlic cloves, peeled*
*24 oil-packed anchovy fillets, rinsed, or 12 salt-packed*
*anchovies, well rinsed and boned*
*3 tbsp olive oil*
*2 tbsp red wine vinegar*
*freshly ground pepper*

### PREPARATION

1 Pound garlic according to taste, using a mortar and pestle. Add the anchovy fillets and continue pounding. Add the olive oil, wine vinegar, and pepper to taste and pound to a coarse paste.
2 Spread the anchovy paste thinly over bruschetta or crostini and serve, or heat through in a 350°F (180°C) oven for 10–15 minutes before serving.

 *This topping can be made in advance and kept in the refrigerator for 2 days. If making in advance, you may want to use less garlic, because the garlic will taste stronger after a day or two.*

## TOMATO & CAPER

*For 18–24 bruschetta or 36–48 crostini*

### INGREDIENTS

*1 small onion, chopped*
*1 tbsp olive oil*
*8 large garlic cloves, finely chopped or crushed*
*2 lb (1 kg) ripe tomatoes, peeled, seeded, and chopped*
*1/2 cup (90 g) capers, rinsed and chopped in a food processor*
*salt and freshly ground pepper*

### PREPARATION

1 Cook the onion in the oil, stirring, for about 5 minutes until tender. Add the garlic and cook, stirring, for about 1 minute, until the garlic begins to color.
2 Add the tomatoes, capers, a small amount of salt, and pepper to taste. Cook over medium heat for 15–20 minutes, stirring often, or until the tomatoes have reduced.
3 Remove the sauce from the heat, taste, and adjust seasonings. Spread over bruschetta or crostini and serve hot.

*This topping can be made in advance and kept in the refrigerator for 2–3 days.*

## TOMATO & MOZZARELLA

*For 18–24 bruschetta or 36–48 crostini*

### INGREDIENTS

*3–4 large garlic cloves, finely chopped or crushed*
*1 tbsp olive oil*
*2 lb (1 kg) tomatoes, peeled, seeded, and chopped*
*pinch of sugar*
*salt, preferably sea salt, and freshly ground pepper*
*1/2 tsp dried thyme (optional)*
*2 tbsp slivered fresh basil*
*1/4 lb (125 g) fresh mozzarella cheese, cut into thin slivers*

### PREPARATION

1 Cook the garlic in the oil until it begins to color, then add the tomatoes, sugar, salt, and dried thyme, if using. Cook, stirring often, for 15–20 minutes, or until the tomatoes have reduced.
2 Stir in the basil and cook for 1 minute. Add pepper to taste and remove the mixture from the heat. Taste, and adjust seasonings.
3 Place a sliver of mozzarella on each bruschetta or crostini, and top with the tomato sauce. Place on a baking sheet and bake in a 375°F (190°C) oven for 5–10 minutes, until the cheese begins to melt. Serve hot.

 *The tomato mixture can be made in advance and kept in the refrigerator.*

---

### *RUSTIC CANAPES*

*Like much of Italian food, bruschetta and crostini derive from an unpretentious rural tradition.*

*Thick, flat slices of Italian country bread, bruschetta originated in antiquity — there are records of them from Roman times. Traditionally, they are grilled over charcoal, then rubbed with garlic, doused with extra-virgin olive oil, and liberally sprinkled with salt and pepper.*

*The word bruschetta actually derives from the Italian* bruscare, *to roast over coals. Bruschetta are always served warm in Italy, either as a snack at any time of day or as an appetizer before the main meal.*

*Crostini, the Italian for croutons, are more delicate than bruschetta and are often fashioned into fancy shapes and buttered before being toasted or baked. Bite-sized crostini are also added to soup.*

*Crostini are particularly popular in the Italian region of Tuscany, where meaty toppings, especially game, are the preferred choice. Crostini with chicken liver topping is one of the region's best-known specialties.*

# CAPONATA

*This sweet and sour vegetable stew from Sicily makes a great topping for bruschetta and crostini.*
*For 18–24 bruschetta or 36–48 crostini*

## INGREDIENTS

*4 ripe fresh tomatoes, or 8 canned Italian plum tomatoes, peeled, seeded, and finely chopped*
*salt and freshly ground pepper*
*2 medium eggplants, peeled and cut into 1/2-in (1-cm) dice, sprinkled with salt for 1 hour*
*2 large red peppers, cored, seeded, and diced*
*2 medium zucchini, diced*
*2 medium onions, chopped*
*4 large garlic cloves, finely chopped or crushed*
*2 heaping tbsp capers, rinsed*
*2 tbsp raisins*
*1 bay leaf*
*1 tsp fresh thyme leaves, or 1/2 tsp dried thyme*
*1/4 cup (60 ml) dry white wine vinegar, sherry vinegar, or cider vinegar*
*1 tbsp sugar*
*2 tbsp olive oil*

## PREPARATION

**1** Combine the tomatoes and a pinch of salt in a pan and cook over low heat, stirring, for 15 minutes. Mash, and set aside.

**2** Rinse the eggplants and dry. Transfer them to an oiled baking dish.

**3** Add the tomatoes, the remaining vegetables, the garlic, capers, raisins, bay leaf, thyme, and salt and pepper to taste. Mix together.

**4** Combine the vinegar and sugar in a saucepan and heat through until the sugar just dissolves. Pour over the vegetables. Add the olive oil and toss together.

**5** Cover the baking dish tightly and bake in a 350°F (180°C) oven for 1 1/2–2 hours, stirring every 30 minutes, until the vegetables are very tender and fragrant. Taste, and adjust seasonings.

**6** Spread the mixture over bruschetta or crostini and serve hot.

 *Caponata will keep for 1 week in the refrigerator.*

# TOMATO CONCASSEE

*For 18–24 bruschetta or 36–48 crostini*

## INGREDIENTS

*1 1/2 lb (750 g) tomatoes, peeled, seeded, and finely chopped*
*1–2 large garlic cloves, finely chopped or crushed*
*1 tbsp balsamic vinegar*
*1 tbsp olive oil*
*2–3 tbsp slivered basil leaves*
*coarse sea salt and freshly ground pepper*

## PREPARATION

**1** Toss together the tomatoes, garlic, vinegar, and oil with the basil and salt and pepper to taste. Let stand for 15 minutes or longer.

**2** Spread the mixture over bruschetta or crostini and serve.

# WILD MUSHROOM

*For 18–24 bruschetta or 36–48 crostini*

## INGREDIENTS

*2 medium shallots, finely chopped*
*2 tbsp olive oil*
*1 lb (500 g) fresh wild mushrooms, cut into 1/4-in (5-mm) slices*
*salt and freshly ground pepper*
*4 large garlic cloves, finely chopped or crushed*
*1/2 cup (30 g) dried cepe mushrooms, soaked and drained (see page 156), coarsely chopped*
*1/4 cup (60 ml) dry white or red wine*
*2 tsp soy sauce*
*2 tsp chopped fresh rosemary*
*1 tsp fresh thyme leaves, or 1/2 tsp dried thyme*

## PREPARATION

**1** Cook the shallots in the oil over medium heat, stirring, for about 5 minutes, until tender.

**2** Add the mushrooms and a little salt and cook, stirring, until they begin to release water, then add the garlic and cepes.

**3** Cook, stirring, for 2 minutes, then add the wine, soy sauce, rosemary, thyme, and pepper to taste. Cook, stirring, for about 10 minutes, until all the liquid has evaporated.

**4** Add 2 tbsp of the soaking liquid from the cepes if the mixture sticks to the pan. Taste, and adjust seasonings. Transfer the mixture to a food processor and chop, pulsing the machine just a few times. Reheat before spreading over bruschetta or crostini.

# WRAPS, ROLLS, & CRISPS

When it comes to impressing guests with beautiful, easy-to-eat finger foods, savory fillings in various types of wrappers or on crispy chips are ideal. The recipes in this section come from far-flung corners of the world. There are phyllo pastries and lemony stuffed grape leaves from Greece and the Middle East, nachos with spicy toppings from Mexico, and sushi, wontons, and soft and crispy spring rolls from the Far East.

# PHYLLO PASTRIES

Paper-thin phyllo is Greek strudel pastry, and the multilayered morsels made with it crumble in the mouth into fragile flakes. I usually make triangles (*tiropites*), but you can also make cigars, or purses and parcels as shown here. Full directions for making these shapes are on pages 142–143. Phyllo pastries freeze well, so you can have them at hand for quick appetizers.

*Pepper*

*Sea salt*

*Feta cheese*

## TO MAKE PHYLLO PASTRIES

*¹/₂ lb (250 g) phyllo pastry makes about 60 pastry shapes*

**1** Make the filling of your choice (see pages 76–77).

**2** Heat ¼ cup (60 ml) olive oil with 4 tbsp (60 g) butter over very low heat until the butter melts.

**3** Take one sheet of phyllo pastry at a time and keep the rest of the pastry wrapped in a damp dish towel so that it does not dry out.

**4** Wrap the phyllo pastry around the filling, following the directions for the different shapes on pages 142–143.

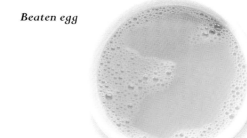

*Beaten egg*

**5** Place the pastries on a nonstick or lightly oiled baking sheet. Brush the tops of the pastries with the remaining oil and butter and bake in a preheated 350°F (180°C) oven for 30 minutes, until golden brown. Serve warm.

 *You can make the fillings and assemble the pastries 1 day in advance, or freeze them uncooked weeks in advance. Bake them only before serving.*
    *To store, place uncooked pastries on an oiled baking sheet, cover, and refrigerate.*
    *To freeze, wrap about 12 uncooked pastries in foil, crimp the edges of the foil tightly, seal in plastic bags, and freeze.*

**Cooking tip:** *If you have frozen the pastries, do not thaw, but transfer directly from the freezer to the oven, brushing them first with a little oil or melted butter. They may require an extra 5–10 minutes of baking time.*

*Rosemary*

*Thyme*

*Parsley*

*Garlic*

**CRISP & CRUMBLY**
*Spinach & Feta Cheese filling is encased in phyllo parcels tied with carrot strips and decorated with cilantro leaves, and in phyllo money bags lightly sprinkled with red paprika.*

*Nutmeg*

*Phyllo pastry*

*Onion*

*Oil*

*Spinach*

# PHYLLO PASTRY FILLINGS

*Phyllo pastries can be filled with an endless variety and combination of fresh-tasting ingredients, which include vegetables, fish, herbs, and cheese — especially Greek feta cheese.*

★

## SPINACH & FETA CHEESE

*Spinach and cheese, a favorite Mediterranean combination, is one of the best-known of Greek savory pastry fillings.
For about 60 pastries*

### INGREDIENTS

*2 lb (1 kg) spinach, stems removed, leaves washed
salt and freshly ground pepper
1 tbsp olive oil
1 medium onion, chopped
3 garlic cloves, finely chopped or crushed
1 bunch flat-leaf parsley, finely chopped
2 tbsp chopped fresh rosemary,
or 2 tsp crumbled dried rosemary
2 tsp fresh thyme leaves, or 1 tsp dried thyme
2 eggs
1/2 lb (250 g) feta cheese, crumbled
pinch of freshly grated nutmeg*

### PREPARATION

**1** Blanch the spinach in a large pan of boiling salted water for 1–2 minutes, or put the spinach in a dry nonstick skillet with only the water left on the leaves after washing. Toss over high heat for 1–2 minutes, until wilted.

**2** Rinse the spinach under cold water, squeeze dry in a dish towel, and chop.

**3** Heat the olive oil over medium heat in a large skillet and add the onion. Cook, stirring, until tender and just beginning to brown.

**4** Add the garlic, stir together for about 30 seconds, then stir in the spinach, parsley, rosemary, and thyme. Remove from the heat.

**5** Beat the eggs in a large bowl and add the feta. Add the spinach mixture and salt and pepper to taste. Stir in the nutmeg and mix everything together well.

## FISH & CILANTRO

*This filling does not keep or freeze well, so make it on the day you bake the pastries.
For about 60 pastries*

### INGREDIENTS

*2 1/2 lb (1.25 kg) cod, whiting, or snapper fillets
1 cup (60 g) chopped cilantro
4 tbsp chopped fresh mint
2 tbsp chopped chives
1 large red pepper, cored, seeded, and finely chopped
2–3 garlic cloves, finely chopped or crushed
juice of 2 large lemons
2 tbsp olive oil
2 eggs, beaten
1/2 tsp ground cumin
salt and freshly ground pepper*

### PREPARATION

**1** Steam the fish for about 7 minutes, until tender. The fish should separate into segments when you pierce it with a fork. Remove from the heat and allow to drain in a colander for 5 minutes.

**2** Transfer the fish to a large bowl and flake the fillets with your fingers or with a fork. Remove all bones – there are always some in cod fillets.

**3** Once you have made sure that all bones have been removed, transfer to a food processor and process for a few seconds until the fish is finely chopped.

**4** Return to the bowl and toss with the remaining ingredients, adding salt and pepper to taste.

---

### *FETA CHEESE*

*Feta cheese is a classic Greek cheese, traditionally made from ewe's milk, although it is now normally made from cow's milk. Because it is preserved in brine, it is sometimes referred to as "pickled cheese." Feta cheese is widely used in Greek and Mediterranean cooking.*

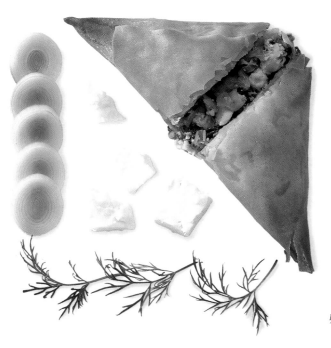

## LAMB & GREEN VEGETABLE

*There is a Middle Eastern influence in this warmly spiced filling of ground lamb with sautéed green vegetables.*
*For about 60 pastries*

### INGREDIENTS

*½ lb (250 g) ground lamb*
*1 tsp ground allspice*
*1 tsp ground nutmeg*
*1 tsp ground cinnamon*
*salt and freshly ground pepper*
*6 tbsp (90 ml) water*
*juice of 1 lemon*
*1 tbsp olive oil*
*2 celery stalks, finely chopped*
*6 scallions, both white and green parts, finely chopped*
*2 leeks, cleaned and finely chopped*
*½ lb (250 g) frozen chopped spinach, thawed and drained*
*4 tbsp finely chopped flat-leaf parsley*

### PREPARATION

1 In a large nonstick skillet, cook the ground lamb for 5 minutes – it will fry in its own fat. Add all the spices, salt to taste, and 1 tsp pepper. Cook, stirring, for another 5 minutes.
2 Add the water and lemon juice and bring to a boil. Simmer for 15 minutes.
3 Meanwhile, in another saucepan, heat the oil and sauté the celery, scallions, and leeks for 5–7 minutes, until softened.
4 Stir in the spinach and heat through. Add the vegetables to the lamb, and then add parsley. Cook for another 10 minutes. Taste, and adjust seasonings.

## LEEK & FETA CHEESE

*The sweet flavor of the leeks, which emerges with gentle cooking, contrasts beautifully with the rich saltiness of feta cheese in this filling.*
*For about 60 pastries*

### INGREDIENTS

*2½ lb (1.25 kg) leeks*
*2 tbsp olive oil*
*1 tsp fresh thyme leaves, or ½ tsp dried thyme*
*freshly ground pepper*
*2 eggs, beaten*
*6 oz (175 g) feta cheese, crumbled*
*½ cup (60 g) freshly grated Parmesan cheese*
*1 bunch flat-leaf parsley, chopped*
*½ cup (30 g) chopped fresh dill*

### PREPARATION

1 Trim the leeks and discard the tough green parts. Split the white parts lengthwise in half, wash thoroughly, and slice thinly.
2 Heat the oil in a large, heavy-bottomed nonstick skillet over medium-low heat and add the leeks. Cook, stirring often, for about 10 minutes, until the leeks are thoroughly tender but not browned. Add the thyme, and salt and pepper to taste. Remove from the heat.
3 Mix together the beaten eggs and feta. Add the leeks and remaining ingredients and stir together well.

*This filling can be made 1–2 days before making the pastries.*

### Quick & Easy Fillings

*If you are short of time, try these simple ideas. They give a delicious – and unusual – Asian flavor to the pastries.*

**SHRIMP & CILANTRO:** Sauté *½ lb (250 g) cooked, peeled shrimp, finely chopped,* with *1 garlic clove, crushed,* in *1 tbsp olive oil* for 5 minutes. Add *2 tbsp finely chopped cilantro, 1 tsp finely grated lime zest,* and *2 tsp lime juice.*
**STIR-FRIED CHICKEN:** Sauté *½ lb (250 g) skinless chicken breast, finely chopped,* with *4 scallions, thinly sliced,* and *2 tsp finely chopped fresh ginger* in *1 tbsp peanut oil.* Mix together in a bowl with *1 tbsp soy sauce, 1 tbsp red or white wine vinegar, 1 tbsp cornstarch,* and *1 tsp sesame oil.*

# DOLMADES

Homemade *dolmades*, or stuffed grape leaves, have a marvelous fresh, tangy flavor. The main ingredients of these leafy parcels are rice and plenty of fresh herbs. Serve them warm or cold.

★

## RICE & HERB DOLMADES

*Makes about 80*

### INGREDIENTS

*3 tbsp olive oil*
*1 medium red or white onion, finely chopped*
*1/4 lb (125 g) scallions,*
*both white and green parts, chopped*
*1 cup (200 g) long-grain rice*
*2–3 garlic cloves, finely chopped or crushed*
*1 tsp ground cumin*
*salt and freshly ground pepper*
*2 cups (500 ml) water*
*1/2 cup (30 g) chopped fresh dill*
*1/2 cup (30 g) chopped flat-leaf parsley*
*1/4 cup (15 g) fresh fennel fronds, chopped*
*4 tbsp chopped fresh mint, or 1 1/2 tsp dried mint*
*1 egg, beaten*
*90 grape leaves (fresh or preserved in brine)*
*juice of 2 large lemons*

### PREPARATION

**1** Heat 2 tbsp of the oil in a large heavy-bottomed skillet, add the onion and scallions, and cook over medium heat for about 5 minutes, stirring, until the onions are translucent.

**2** Add the rice and cook for 3–5 minutes, stirring, until very lightly browned. Stir in garlic to taste, the cumin, 1/2 tsp salt, and the water. Bring to a boil and simmer for 10 minutes, until the water has been absorbed. The rice will not be cooked through. Remove from the heat and let cool.

**3** Stir in the herbs with salt and pepper to taste. Add the egg and combine well.

**4** If using preserved grape leaves, rinse them well. Bring a large pan of water to a rolling boil and drop in the grape leaves, several at a time. Blanch preserved grape leaves for about 30 seconds, fresh leaves for 3–5 minutes, until softened. Remove and drain well in a colander or on paper towels.

**5** Brush the bottom of a wide, heavy-bottomed saucepan with the remaining oil. Add about 3 tbsp water and cover with a layer of grape leaves, glossy side down. Use any torn leaves for this.

**6** Snip off the stems of the remaining grape leaves and assemble the dolmades by filling and folding them as directed on page 79.

**7** Place the dolmades seam side down in the pan, on top of the layer of leaves, and squeeze them together in tightly packed layers. Pour over the lemon juice, then pour in enough water to cover.

**8** Place a small plate on top to keep the dolmades intact while cooking, then cover the pan with a lid. Bring to a boil over medium heat, reduce the heat, and simmer for 2 hours, until the grape leaves are tender.

**9** Carefully remove the dolmades from the water with a slotted spoon and allow to drain on racks set over plates, for 15 minutes or longer.

### VARIATION

**RICE & MEAT DOLMADES:** Substitute the following filling for the filling in the main recipe: Cook *1 medium onion, finely chopped*, in *2 tbsp olive oil*, stirring, for about 5 minutes, until translucent. Add *1/2 lb (250 g) lean ground lamb* and cook, stirring, until browned. Break up the meat with the back of a wooden spoon so that it does not form lumps. Add *1 cup (200 g) long-grain rice*, *2–3 garlic cloves, finely chopped or crushed*, *1 tsp ground allspice*, and *1 tsp ground cumin*. Cook for about 3 minutes, stirring, until the rice just begins to toast. Turn the heat to low and stir in *1 1/2 cups (350 ml) water*. Bring to a boil and simmer for 10 minutes, or until the water has been absorbed. The rice will not be cooked through. Remove from the heat and let cool. Stir in *4 tbsp chopped fresh mint, 1/2 cup (30 g) chopped parsley, and salt and freshly ground pepper to taste*. Add *1 egg, beaten*, and combine well. Make the dolmades following steps 4–9 above.

**PRETTY PARCELS**
*Rice & Herb Dolmades are tied with leek and pepper strips and garnished with Cucumber Twists (see page 155) and lemon.*

## FILLING & FOLDING DOLMADES

*1* Lay a leaf glossy side down (vein side up) with the stem end nearest to you. Place 1 heaping tsp of filling in the middle of the leaf.

*2* Fold one side of the leaf over the filling and then fold the other side of the leaf over the filling.

*3* Roll the leaf tightly from the stem end. Repeat with the remaining leaves and filling. The stuffed leaves should form 1-in (2.5-cm) long parcels.

# NACHOS

Add spice to any party by serving nachos – crunchy nacho chips topped with exciting Latin-American flavors. Nacho chips are made from tortillas cut into bite-sized chips or pieces and deep-fried. You can use ready-made nacho chips which come in different shapes, if you don't want to deep-fry your own tortilla chips. However, homemade chips are infinitely better than most commercial chips, which tend to be oversalted and quite oily. Make nacho chips well in advance and store them in airtight cans. You can also serve bowls of homemade nacho chips on their own to accompany drinks and dips. Some nachos are served cold, others hot. To create full-flavored meat, fish, and vegetable toppings for mouth-watering nachos, see pages 82–83.

*Guacamole & Tomato Nachos*

*Guacamole & Tomato Nachos*

*Smoked Salmon Nachos*

## TO MAKE NACHO CHIPS

*Makes 48 chips*

**1** Cut 12 corn tortillas into quarters. Heat 1 quart (1 liter) canola or sunflower oil in a wide saucepan or deep-fat fryer to 350°F (180°C).

**2** Deep-fry the tortilla quarters in batches of 4–8. They should float to the top and turn golden brown in seconds. Remove immediately with a skimmer or slotted spoon and drain on paper towels.

**3** Allow the oil to reheat to 350°F (180°C) between batches to maintain the correct temperature. When all of the chips are done, salt them lightly.

**LIGHT & SPICY**
*Guacamole & Tomato Nachos and Black Bean Nachos evoke the true taste of Latin America, while Smoked Salmon Nachos and Chicken Nachos provide a contrast with milder flavors.*

**Black Bean Nachos**

**Chicken Nachos**

**Smoked Salmon Nachos**

# BLACK BEAN NACHOS

*This is a popular Mexican dish, which I make extra thick when I am using it as a topping for nacho chips.*
*Makes 48*

## INGREDIENTS

*2 tbsp canola or sunflower oil*
*1 large onion, chopped*
*4 large garlic cloves, finely chopped or crushed*
*2 cups (375 g) dried black beans, soaked overnight in 3 quarts (3 liters) water*
*2 quarts (2 liters) water*
*salt*
*2 tbsp chopped cilantro*
*2 tsp ground cumin*
*2 tsp chili powder*
*48 nacho chips*
*1 cup (125 g) grated Cheddar cheese*
*6 tbsp (90 ml) crème fraîche or plain nonfat yogurt*
*Green Tomatillo Salsa (see page 47) or chopped tomatillos*
*cilantro for garnish*

## PREPARATION

1 Heat half the oil in a large, heavy-bottomed saucepan and sauté the onion with a quarter of the garlic for about 3 minutes, until the onion begins to soften.

2 Drain the beans and add to the pan with the 2 quarts (2 liters) water. Add another quarter of the garlic, and bring to a boil. Reduce the heat, cover, and simmer for 1 hour.

3 Add salt to taste, the remaining garlic, and the cilantro, and simmer for about 1 hour, until the beans are soft and the liquid has thickened and become aromatic.

4 Let cool, then drain off about two-thirds of the liquid, and reserve. Mash half the bean mixture coarsely in a food processor or with a potato masher in batches. Stir back into the remaining bean mixture.

5 Heat the remaining oil in a large nonstick pan over medium-high heat, and add the cumin, chili powder, and a pinch of salt. Cook until the spices begin to sizzle, then add the beans. (This can be done in batches if your pan is not large enough to hold all the beans together.)

6 Fry the beans for 15–20 minutes, mashing with the back of a wooden spoon and stirring often, until they begin to get crusty and aromatic. If they seem too dry, add some of the reserved cooking liquid. The beans should bubble, thicken, and reduce, forming a thin crust on the bottom of the pan, which you should stir back into the mixture.

7 Place the nacho chips on baking sheets and sprinkle with the grated cheese. Place in a 375°F (190°C) oven for 5–10 minutes, until the cheese melts.

8 Spread the refried beans over the cheese, and top with crème fraîche or yogurt and salsa or chopped tomatillos. Garnish with cilantro.

## Quick Nacho Toppings

*For a quick snack, top nacho chips with an assortment of tasty ingredients, most of which are readily available from supermarkets or delicatessens, or which have been prepared in advance. Here are some suggestions:*

**SMOKED SALMON:** *Diced avocado and tomatoes topped with smoked salmon and garnished with onion slivers and sprigs of fresh dill.*

**SHRIMP & TOMATO:** *Fresh Tomato Salsa (see page 29) and cooked, peeled shrimp, garnished with lime and sprigs of fresh dill.*

**CHICKEN:** *Shredded cooked chicken tossed with finely diced celery or scallion and plain nonfat yogurt or sour cream, and garnished with slivers of red pepper.*

**SEVICHE:** *Seviche (see page 104), made with very finely chopped fish and vegetables and drained, garnished with chopped cilantro.*

**Shrimp & Tomato Nachos**

# GUACAMOLE NACHOS

*My guacamole is mild, with no hot chilis added to it. The spicy flavor comes from the salsa which garnishes each nacho chip.*
*Makes 48*

## INGREDIENTS

4 large ripe avocados
2 medium tomatoes, chopped
2 tbsp finely chopped red onion
1 small garlic clove, finely chopped or crushed
juice of 1–2 lemons
1/4–1/2 tsp ground cumin
1/4–1/2 tsp chili powder
salt
48 nacho chips
3/4 cup (90 g) grated mild Cheddar cheese
1/2 cup (125 ml) plain nonfat yogurt, fromage blanc
(see page 156), or crème fraîche
1/2 recipe Fresh Tomato Salsa (see page 29)
radishes for garnish

## PREPARATION

1 Cut the avocados in half, remove the pits, and scoop out the flesh with a spoon. Mash the flesh in a bowl with a wooden spoon, or using a mortar and pestle. Add the chopped tomatoes and continue to mash together.
2 Add the onion and garlic, with lemon juice, cumin, chili powder, and salt to taste. Cover and refrigerate until you are ready to assemble the nachos.
3 Place the nacho chips on baking sheets and sprinkle with the grated cheese. Place in a 375°F (190°C) oven for 5–10 minutes, until the cheese melts.
4 Place a spoonful of guacamole on each chip, then a little yogurt, fromage blanc, or crème fraîche, and a spoonful of salsa. Garnish with radishes.

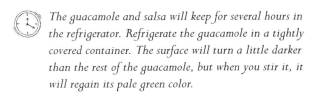

*The guacamole and salsa will keep for several hours in the refrigerator. Refrigerate the guacamole in a tightly covered container. The surface will turn a little darker than the rest of the guacamole, but when you stir it, it will regain its pale green color.*

## VARIATION

**GUACAMOLE & TOMATO:** Arrange *chopped tomato and avocado* on top of the guacamole instead of the yogurt, fromage blanc, or crème fraîche, and the salsa. Garnish the nachos with *cilantro* instead of radishes.

# CHICKEN NACHOS WITH SALSA VERDE

*Makes 48*

## INGREDIENTS

1 medium onion, coarsely chopped
2 garlic cloves, crushed
1 1/2 quarts (1.5 liters) water
salt and freshly ground pepper
2 large whole chicken breasts, total weight
about 1 1/4 lb (625 g), halved
1/2 tsp dried thyme
1/2 tsp dried oregano or marjoram
2 bay leaves
Green Tomatillo Salsa (see page 47)
4 tbsp chopped cilantro
48 nacho chips
3/4 cup (175 ml) crème fraîche, fromage blanc (see
page 156), or plain nonfat yogurt
1 large or 2 small avocados, peeled and diced
juice of 1 large lime
additional cilantro for garnish

## PREPARATION

1 Combine the onion, garlic, water, and 1 tsp salt in a large, heavy-bottomed saucepan and bring to a boil. Add the chicken. Skim off any foam that rises, then add the thyme, oregano or marjoram, and bay leaves. Reduce the heat, cover partially, and simmer for 15 minutes.
2 Remove from the heat and let the chicken cool in the broth. Remove the chicken from the broth, and skin, bone, and shred the meat.
3 Strain the stock through a cheesecloth-lined strainer and set aside for another purpose.
4 Toss the shredded chicken with the tomatillo salsa, chopped cilantro, and salt and pepper to taste.
5 Place 1 heaping tsp of the mixture on each nacho chip, and top with a little crème fraîche, fromage blanc, or yogurt.
6 Toss together the diced avocado and lime juice, and add salt to taste. Place about 2 tsp of the mixture on top of each nacho chip, and garnish with cilantro.

# SUSHI ROLLS

Sushi rolls are a delight. They look beautiful and are delicious. The only special items you will need are a bamboo rolling mat, a wooden rice paddle (conventional wooden spoons can be used instead), Japanese style rice, and *nori*, which is dried seaweed.

★

## CALIFORNIA SUSHI

*This is a fresh variation of the classic Japanese sushi.*
*Makes about 70 slices*

### INGREDIENTS

1 1/2 cups (375 g) Japanese style short-grain rice
1/4 cup (60 ml) seasoned rice vinegar (see page 156)
1/2 cup (125 ml) water mixed with 1 tbsp rice vinegar
(for dipping paddle or spoons, and hands)
8 sheets nori
2–3 ripe but firm avocados, peeled, cut into 1/4-in (5-mm)
wide strips, and tossed in juice of 1/2 lemon
24 cooked, peeled shrimp, cut in half lengthwise,
then crosswise

### PREPARATION

1 Make the vinegared rice: Rinse the rice until the water runs clear. Leave to soak in a saucepan for 15 minutes.
2 Cover the pan tightly and bring to a boil. Simmer for 5–10 minutes, until the rice hisses at the bottom of the pan. Do not uncover. Turn off the heat and let stand, covered, for 30 minutes.
3 Transfer the rice to a wide bowl and toss, using a flat, wooden rice paddle or 2 wooden spoons, until cool. When no more steam rises from the rice, gradually fold in the seasoned vinegar, 1 tbsp at a time. Dip the paddle or spoons in the water and vinegar mixture so that the rice does not stick to them. Cover the rice with a damp dish towel until ready to use. Do not refrigerate.
4 If the nori sheets are green, they have been toasted already. If they are black, toast them by fanning them over an open flame or a hot burner, until just bright green. This happens in seconds.
5 Place each nori sheet, shiny side down, on a bamboo rolling mat. Moisten a measuring spoon with the water and vinegar mixture and spread 4–5 tbsp of the rice on each sheet (see page 85).
6 Lay the avocado strips along the middle of the rice and cover with pieces of shrimp. Roll up the nori around the filling as directed on page 85, then cut each roll into 3/4-in (2-cm) slices.

## CUCUMBER SUSHI

*This traditional sushi roll is known as* kapa maki
*in Japanese.*
*Makes about 70 slices*

### INGREDIENTS

1 1/2 cups (375 g) Japanese style short-grain rice
1/4 cup (60 ml) seasoned rice vinegar (see page 156)
1/2 cup (125 ml) water mixed with 1 tbsp rice vinegar
(for dipping paddle or spoons and hands)
8 sheets nori
1–2 tsp wasabi (Japanese horseradish)
4 tsp sesame seeds, lightly toasted
3 oz (90 g) sliced pickled ginger
1 cucumber, seeded and cut into 1/4-in
(5-mm) wide strips

### PREPARATION

1 Make the vinegared rice and prepare the nori as directed in steps 1–5 of California Sushi, left.
2 Spread 1/8–1/4 tsp wasabi in a line along the middle of the rice on each sheet of nori.
3 Sprinkle 1/2 tsp sesame seeds over each line of wasabi. Arrange some pickled ginger and cucumber strips side-by-side on top of the sesame seeds.
4 Roll up the nori around the cucumber and ginger filling as directed on page 85, then cut each roll into 3/4-in (2-cm) slices.

### TRADITIONAL SUSHI

*Sushi is a popular Japanese snack based on rice flavored with rice vinegar and shaped into balls, squares, or rolls. Traditionally, the rice is wrapped around a filling of raw fish or vegetables seasoned with a fiery horseradish paste called* wasabi. *Pickles are added, then the whole is rolled in thin sheets of* nori *or dried seaweed. Sushi is fun — and healthy. Apart from the filling, the seaweed itself is a good source of vitamins and minerals.*

**EAST MEETS WEST**

*A platter of California Sushi — Japanese rice rolls with a West Coast accent — is garnished with Pickled Ginger Roses (see page 155) on Cucumber Fences (see page 154).*

## FILLING & ROLLING NORI

*1* *Spread the rice on the nori in a $^{1}/4$-in (5-mm) layer. Leave a 1-in (2.5-cm) margin at the top and bottom. Place the filling on the rice.*

*2* *Lift up the mat and nori and fold them away from you over the filling. Press down and roll up the nori, lifting the mat as you go to avoid rolling it in.*

*Nori*

*Wasabi*

# A Feast
# from Asia

*Throw your own mini Asian banquet with Japanese sushi, Chinese crispy
spring rolls, Vietnamese soft spring rolls, and Indonesian saté, served with
dipping sauces. Crown it all with a refreshing Asian
fruit platter filled with exotic tropical fruits.*

**Bottled hoisin sauce**

**Soy sauce sprinkled with sesame seeds**

*California Sushi
(page 84) with
shrimp and
pickled ginger*

Asian Fruit
Platter
(page 132)

Coconut Tuiles (page 127)

Soft Spring Rolls (pages 90–93) and
Crispy Spring Rolls (page 94)

Chicken Saté
(page 98)

# WONTONS

Deep-fried or poached, wontons make irresistible party food. Spinach and tofu are two of my favorite healthy ingredients for fillings, but you can also use any of the spring roll fillings (see pages 92–94).

★

## SPINACH & TOFU WONTONS

*This recipe is for deep-fried wontons; if you prefer them poached, drop about 10 wontons at a time into 2 quarts (2 liters) boiling chicken or vegetable stock, poach for about 4 minutes, until al dente, then remove with a slotted spoon. Serve hot or cold on toothpicks.*
*Makes 40*

### INGREDIENTS

¾ *lb (375 g) fresh spinach, stems removed, leaves washed, or a 10-oz (300 g) package frozen spinach, thawed, excess moisture squeezed out*
*salt*
*1 tbsp canola or sunflower oil, more for deep-frying*
*6 scallions, both white and green parts, chopped*
*1 large garlic clove, finely chopped or crushed*
*1 tsp grated fresh ginger*
½ *lb (250 g) firm tofu, cut into small dice*
*2 tbsp sesame seeds*
*2–3 tbsp soy sauce*
*2 tsp dry sherry*
*4 tbsp chopped cilantro*
*40 wonton wrappers*
*1 egg, beaten, or 1 tbsp cornstarch or arrowroot dissolved in a little water*
*dipping sauce of your choice (see right and page 94)*

### PREPARATION

1 If using fresh spinach, blanch it in boiling salted water for 1–2 minutes or, put it in a dry nonstick skillet with only the water left on the leaves after washing. Toss over high heat for 1–2 minutes, until wilted.
2 Rinse the spinach under cold water, squeeze dry in a dish towel, and chop.
3 Heat the oil in a wok or large nonstick skillet, add the scallions, garlic, and ginger, and stir-fry for 3 minutes, until the scallions begin to soften.
4 Add the diced tofu and sesame seeds and stir-fry for 3–5 minutes over medium-high heat.
5 Add the spinach and stir-fry for another minute. Add the soy sauce and sherry and continue to stir-fry over medium heat for 5 minutes.

6 Increase the heat and cook, stirring, until all the liquid evaporates. Remove from the heat and stir in the cilantro. Taste, and adjust seasonings.
7 Finely chop the mixture either by hand or for just a second or two in a food processor. Fill the wontons as directed on page 89, sealing them with the beaten egg, or the cornstarch or arrowroot dissolved in a little water.
8 Pour oil into a wok or deep-fat fryer up to a depth of 4 in (10 cm) and heat to 350°F (180°C). Deep-fry the wontons in batches of 6 until golden brown, turning them to color them evenly. Remove with a slotted spoon and drain on paper towels. Allow the oil to reheat to 350°F (180°C) between each batch. Serve hot with a dipping sauce of your choice.

### Quick Dipping Sauce

*This sauce goes particularly well with wontons, but you can serve them with any of the dipping sauces on page 94.*

Combine ½ *cup (125 ml) water* with ¼ *cup (60 ml) each soy sauce and sake or dry sherry. Heat just to boiling and add 4 tsp finely chopped or grated fresh ginger and 1 small red chili, cored, seeded, and finely chopped (optional).*

---

### CHINESE PARCELS

*Wontons are small Chinese dumplings made of paper-thin pastry, filled with a chopped or ground mixture of meat, sea food, or vegetables. You could make your own wonton wrappers from a dough of flour, salt, water, and eggs, rolled out to wafer thinness. Still, it is easier to buy fresh or frozen ready-made wonton wrappers, from Chinese food shops. If you cannot buy wonton wrappers, use two or three layers of phyllo pastry squares (see pages 142–143).*

*Once made, wontons are very versatile and take well to deep-frying, poaching, or steaming. They are usually served with a chili and garlic or some other spicy sauce.*

**GOLDEN WONDER**
*Spinach & Tofu Wontons
are accompanied by
Quick Dipping Sauce.*

## FILLING WONTONS

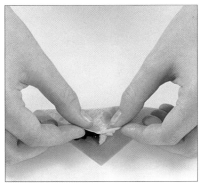

*1* Place 1 tsp of filling in the middle of a wonton wrapper. Brush the edges with beaten egg, or the cornstarch or arrowroot and water mixture.

*2* Fold the wrapper diagonally over the filling to form a triangle. Firmly press the edges together to seal.

*3* Join the two bottom ends of the triangle together at their tips and seal. Repeat with the remaining wrappers and filling.

# SOFT SPRING ROLLS

These are very fresh rolls made with rice-flour wrappers that need no cooking, just a quick soak to soften them. They are lighter than the deep-fried Crispy Spring Rolls (see page 94) and much healthier. There are two sizes of rice-flour wrappers available at Asian specialty shops; I use the small ones for parties.

*Garlic*

## TO MAKE SOFT SPRING ROLLS

**1** Prepare your choice of filling from the recipes given on pages 92–93.

**2** Place 1 x 6-in (15-cm) rice-flour wrapper at a time in a bowl of hot water for about 30 seconds, until just softened.

*Scallion*

**3** Using 1 heaping tbsp of filling for each wrapper, make up each roll as directed below. Refrigerate, covered, until ready to serve.

*Ginger*

**4** Arrange the spring rolls on a large platter as illustrated here and garnish with Carrot Flowers (see page 155), Radish Roses and Scallion Curls (see page 149), chopped cilantro, and finely chopped radish and carrot. Serve with a dipping sauce (see pages 88 and 94), if you like.

*Oil*

**SUBTLE DIFFERENCES**
*Light and fresh, Vegetarian Soft Spring Rolls (see page 93) contain crunchy vegetables, such as green pepper, scallion, carrot, and bean sprouts, which contrast with the soft wrapper.*

## FILLING & ROLLING A SOFT SPRING ROLL

*Carrot*

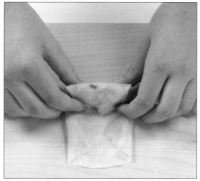

*Chinese
mushroom*

**1** *Place the filling in the middle of the rice-flour wrapper, slightly nearer to the edge closest to you.*

**2** *Fold the sides of the wrapper over the filling, then roll the wrapper up tightly around the filling.*

*Cellophane
noodles*

Green
pepper

*Cilantro*

Soy sauce

Rice
vinegar

Salt

# FILLINGS FOR SOFT SPRING ROLLS

*I choose ingredients with contrasting textures and colors to fill these spring rolls.
They complement the soft translucent wrappers beautifully.
All the fillings can be made a day in advance and kept chilled.*

★

## CRUNCHY TOFU

*To fill 20–25 x 6-in (15-cm) rice-flour wrappers*

### INGREDIENTS

8 medium Chinese dried mushrooms
2 tbsp grated fresh ginger
2 tbsp peanut or canola oil
12 scallions, white and green parts, chopped
2 garlic cloves, finely chopped or crushed
½ lb (250 g) firm tofu, cut into small dice
2 tbsp soy sauce
1 tbsp dry sherry
3 medium carrots, shredded
½ medium head green cabbage, shredded
6 oz (175 g) bean sprouts, chopped
1 red pepper, cored, seeded, and finely chopped
½ cup (30 g) chopped cilantro

### PREPARATION

1 Soak the mushrooms in boiling water for
30 minutes, until tender. Rinse in several
changes of water and squeeze dry. Cut away the
stems and discard. Cut the caps into thin slivers.
2 Stir-fry the ginger in the oil for 30 seconds, or
until the ginger just begins to color. Add the
scallions and stir-fry until they begin to soften.
Add the mushrooms, garlic, and tofu.
3 Stir-fry for 1–2 minutes, then add the soy sauce
and sherry. Stir-fry for 1 minute, then add the
remaining vegetables. Remove from the heat and
add the cilantro. Taste, and adjust seasonings.

## SHRIMP & CILANTRO

*This easy filling is particularly light and refreshing, and it
requires no cooking if you use ready-cooked shrimp — just
combine all the ingredients together.
To fill 20 x 6-in (15-cm) rice-flour wrappers*

### INGREDIENTS

2 oz (60 g) cellophane noodles
1 lb (500 g) shrimp, cooked, peeled, deveined, and
cut in half crosswise
1 cup (60 g) chopped cilantro
½ cup (30 g) slivered fresh mint leaves
8 medium Romaine lettuce leaves,
washed, dried, and shredded
¼ cup (60 ml) lime juice
1 tbsp sesame oil
2–3 tsp grated fresh ginger
soy sauce or salt
freshly ground pepper

### PREPARATION

1 Soak the noodles in boiling water for 20–30
minutes, until the noodles are tender. Drain
and break them apart. Cut them into pieces
approximately 2 in (5 cm) long, using scissors.
2 Combine with the remaining ingredients. Adjust
the soy sauce or salt to taste and toss together.

### SOFT SPRING ROLLS

*Soft spring rolls are also known as Vietnamese spring rolls.
Because the rice-flour wrapper is translucent, colorful
filling ingredients clearly show through, which makes the
rolls very appealing. Rice-flour wrappers are easy to work
with and should be soaked in hot water before use to make
them flexible when rolling. To prevent them from drying
out, it is best to work with one sheet at a time. Soft spring
rolls are usually served cold with a spicy dipping sauce to
complement the filling. (See pages 88 and 94 for dipping
sauce recipes.)*

*Cilantro*

*Fresh ginger*

*Tofu*

# VEGETARIAN

*To keep the vegetables crunchy, make sure
not to overcook them.
To fill 40–45 x 6-in (15-cm) rice-flour wrappers*

### INGREDIENTS

*3 oz (90 g) cellophane noodles
1 quart (1 liter) boiling water
8 medium dried Chinese mushrooms
3 medium carrots
2 tbsp peanut or canola oil
2 tbsp grated fresh ginger
12 scallions, both white and green parts, chopped
2 garlic cloves, finely chopped or crushed
1 green pepper, cored, seeded, and finely chopped
6 oz (175 g) bean sprouts, chopped
½ cup (30 g) chopped cilantro
2 tbsp soy sauce
1 tbsp rice vinegar
salt and freshly ground pepper*

### PREPARATION

1 Put the cellophane noodles in a bowl and pour on the boiling water. Let stand 30 minutes, until tender.
2 While the noodles are softening, soak the mushrooms. Place in a bowl and pour on boiling water to cover. Let stand 30 minutes, until tender. Drain and rinse in several changes of water. Squeeze dry. Cut away the stems and discard. Cut the caps into thin slivers.
3 Drain the noodles and cut into 1-in (2.5-cm) lengths with scissors. Cut the carrots into 1-in (2.5-cm) matchsticks.
4 Heat half the oil in a wok or a large, heavy-bottomed nonstick skillet over medium heat and add the ginger. Cook for about 30 seconds until it just begins to color. Then add the scallions, garlic, and slivered mushrooms. Stir together for 1 minute and transfer to a bowl.
5 Add the remaining oil to the wok or skillet and heat over medium-high heat. Add the carrots, green pepper, and bean sprouts. Stir together for 2–3 minutes, until the vegetables are crisp-tender.
6 Add the noodles, cilantro, soy sauce, vinegar, and salt and pepper to taste. Stir together and remove from heat. Taste, and adjust seasonings.

# SMOKED DUCK

*You can put together this luscious filling in no time.
To fill 32 x 6-in (15-cm) rice-flour wrappers*

### INGREDIENTS

*2 cucumbers
½ tsp salt, plus salt for cucumber
2 tbsp rice vinegar
2 tbsp sesame oil
¼ cup (60 ml) bottled plum sauce
¾ lb (375 g) smoked duck breast, cut into thin slivers
12 scallions, both white and green parts, shredded
2 tbsp chopped fresh mint*

### PREPARATION

1 Shred the cucumbers, sprinkle with salt, and toss. Let stand for 15 minutes in a strainer set over a bowl. Rinse thoroughly and squeeze dry.
2 Stir together the vinegar and ½ tsp salt. When the salt has dissolved, stir in the sesame oil and half the plum sauce.
3 Toss the slivers of duck breast with the remaining plum sauce.
4 In a large bowl, combine the cucumber, plum sauce and vinegar mixture, duck breast, scallions, and mint. Toss together well.

# CRISPY SPRING ROLLS

*These crispy Chinese rolls are surprisingly easy to make. Ready-made spring roll wrappers are available in Asian food stores.*

★

## PORK OR CHICKEN CRISPY SPRING ROLLS

*Makes 30–40 rolls*

### INGREDIENTS

*3 tbsp soy sauce*
*1 tbsp sesame oil*
*1 tbsp water*
*1 tsp sherry*
*1/4 tsp sugar*
*salt and freshly ground pepper*
*3/4 lb (375 g) lean pork, or chicken breast, or*
*a combination, cut into slivers*
*2 tbsp peanut or canola oil, more for deep-frying*
*2 tbsp grated fresh ginger*
*12 scallions, both white and green parts, chopped*
*2 garlic cloves, finely chopped or crushed*
*1/2 lb (250 g) snow peas, trimmed and cut into thirds*
*6 oz (175 g) bean sprouts, chopped*
*1 red pepper, cored, seeded, and finely chopped*
*1/2 cup (30 g) chopped cilantro*
*1 tbsp rice vinegar*
*30–40 spring roll wrappers*
*1 tbsp arrowroot or cornstarch*
*dipping sauce of your choice (see right)*

### PREPARATION

1 Mix together 1 tbsp of the soy sauce, the sesame oil, water, sherry, sugar, 1/4 tsp salt, and pepper to taste. Toss with the meat and marinate for 30 minutes, stirring once or twice.
2 Heat half the oil in a wok or a heavy-bottomed nonstick skillet over medium heat. Add the ginger. Cook for about 30 seconds, until the ginger just begins to color.
3 Add the scallions, garlic, and the meat with its marinade. Stir-fry briefly, until the meat is cooked through. Transfer to a bowl.
4 Add the remaining oil to the pan and heat over medium-high heat. Stir-fry the snow peas, bean sprouts, and red pepper for 2–3 minutes, until the vegetables are crisp-tender.
5 Stir in the cilantro, the remaining soy sauce, the rice vinegar, and salt and pepper to taste. Remove from the heat and toss with the meat mixture. Taste, and adjust seasonings.

6 Place a spring roll wrapper diagonally on the work surface so that it appears diamond-shaped in front of you rather than square. Place 1 tbsp filling on the wrapper near the bottom corner.
7 Fold the sides in over the filling, then fold the bottom corner over this and roll tightly, away from you. Seal each roll with the arrowroot or cornstarch dissolved in a little water.
8 Fill a wok or deep fryer with oil to a depth of 4 in (10 cm) and heat to 350°F (180°C). Deep-fry the rolls in batches until golden brown, turning them to brown them evenly (this should only take a couple of minutes). Remove and drain on paper towels. Let the oil reheat to 350°F (180°C) between each batch. Serve with a dipping sauce of your choice.

*These rolls are best served hot. If they have cooled before serving, reheat the oil to 350°F (180°C) and crisp the rolls in the hot oil. The fillings can be made the day before you make the rolls, although they will lose some texture.*

### Dipping Sauces

*Serve wontons, soft spring rolls, and crispy spring rolls with either or both of these dipping sauces. Just combine all the ingredients in a bowl. You could also serve the Quick Dipping Sauce (see page 88) or bottled hoisin or plum sauce for those who like sweet flavors, or soy sauce.*

**TERIYAKI SAUCE:** Combine *1/4 cup (60 ml) tamari soy sauce, 1/4 cup (60 ml) sake or dry sherry, 2 tbsp mild honey, 1 tbsp grated fresh ginger (or 1/2 tsp ground ginger), 2 garlic cloves, finely chopped or crushed, 1 tbsp sesame oil, and 1/4 tsp mustard powder.*
**TAHINI–TAMARI SAUCE:** Combine *1/4 cup (60 ml) tamari soy sauce, 1/2 cup (125 ml) sesame tahini, 1 tsp grated fresh ginger, 2 tsp dry sherry,* and enough hot water to thin out the sauce to the desired consistency.

# FISH, MEAT, & POULTRY

In France, a buffet that features high-protein items, such as pâtés, fish, and chicken, is referred to as a buffet renforcé, one that is fortified with satisfying dishes. Meat and fish dishes add substance to a buffet, and this is important if it is likely to be the main meal for your guests. It's also a good idea to serve at least one high-protein item when people may be drinking alcohol over the course of a few hours.

# KEBABS & MEATBALLS

Broiled bite-sized food on skewers are featured in many cuisines – for example, Middle Eastern kebabs, Asian saté, and Mediterranean brochettes. Fish, sea food, lean meat and poultry, and vegetables can all be skewered and broiled or barbecued – the marinade will determine the accent. If broiling or grilling fish, use firm, slightly oily fish, such as tuna and swordfish.

**SAVORY SKEWERS**
*Middle Eastern Meatballs surround Chicken & Pepper Kebabs and Shrimp & Baby Corn Kebabs, with Tahini-Yogurt Dip in a green pepper cup.*

## TO MAKE KEBABS OR MEATBALLS

**1** Prepare meatballs (see page 99) or cut fish, meat, or poultry into strips or 1-in (2.5-cm) cubes, and toss in marinade according to recipe (see pages 98–99). Refrigerate for the time given in individual recipes. Stir the mixture from time to time to redistribute the marinade.

**2** If using wooden skewers for the kebabs, soak them in water for at least 30 minutes to prevent them from burning while broiling.

**3** Thread the marinated ingredients on skewers. Grill the kebabs or meatballs on a prepared outdoor barbecue, under a broiler, or in a 375°F (190°C) oven for the time given in the recipe, basting every 2 minutes with the marinade. Serve with dipping sauces of your choice (see pages 28–29 and 99).

*Middle Eastern Meatballs*

## CHICKEN & PEPPER KEBABS

*Makes about 25*

### INGREDIENTS

*3 whole chicken breasts, skinned, boned, and halved*
*3 garlic cloves, peeled*
*salt and freshly ground pepper*
*seeds from 10 cardamom pods*
*1/2 tsp ground allspice*
*1/2 tsp ground cinnamon*
*1/2 tsp ground cumin*
*5 tbsp (75 ml) plain nonfat yogurt*
*juice of 3 large limes*
*3 tbsp olive oil*
*3 medium peppers (red, yellow, and green),*
*cored, seeded, and cut into 3/4-in (2-cm) squares*

### PREPARATION

**1** Cut the chicken into 1-in (2.5-cm) pieces and place in a bowl.

**2** Pound the garlic with 1/4 tsp salt using a mortar and pestle. Grind the cardamom seeds in a spice grinder (or pound using a mortar and pestle), and add to the garlic with the other spices and 1/4 tsp ground pepper. Mix together with the yogurt, lime juice, and olive oil.

**3** Add the marinade to the chicken and stir well. Refrigerate for at least 2 hours, stirring occasionally.

**4** Thread the chicken onto about 25 x 5-in (12-cm) skewers, with pepper squares at either end. Barbecue or broil for 4–6 minutes, or cook in a 375°F (190°C) oven for 5–10 minutes, basting every 2 minutes with the marinade.

**5** Serve with any dip of your choice (see page 99).

### VARIATIONS

**SHRIMP & BABY CORN KEBABS:** Substitute *2 lb (1 kg) large shrimp, peeled and deveined,* for the chicken and *20 baby corn, cut into 1/2-in (1-cm) pieces,* for the green and yellow peppers. Halve the red pepper squares into triangles. Marinate the shrimp for 30 minutes only. Thread 1 shrimp between 2 corn pieces and top with a red pepper triangle. Broil for 2 minutes, turning often. Serve hot or cold.

**SHRIMP & PEPPER KEBABS:** Substitute *2 lb (1 kg) large shrimp, peeled and deveined,* for the chicken. Cut *1 green and 1 yellow pepper* into 1-in (2.5-cm) pieces. Marinate the shrimp for 30 minutes. Thread shrimp and pepper onto skewers and broil for 2 minutes. Garnish with chopped parsley.

## BEEF & CHICKEN SATE

*You can make these Indonesian style kebabs with all chicken or all beef, if you prefer not to mix the two meats together.*
*Makes about 25*

### INGREDIENTS

*1/2 lb (250 g) tender beef steak*
*1/2 lb (250 g) skinless, boned chicken breast*

**FOR THE MARINADE**
*2 tbsp soy sauce*
*1 tbsp white wine vinegar*
*1 tbsp canola or sunflower oil*
*1 tsp ground coriander*
*1 tsp ground cumin*
*1 tsp chili powder*
*1 tsp ground ginger*
*1 tsp sugar*

**FOR THE PEANUT SAUCE**
*1 1/2 tbsp canola or sunflower oil*
*1 1/2 cups (175 g) unsalted roasted peanuts, ground*
*2 garlic cloves, finely chopped*
*1/2 tsp crushed dried red chilis*
*1 tsp ground ginger*
*1 tsp brown sugar*
*salt*
*1 tbsp lemon juice*
*1 1/2 cups (350 ml) chicken stock*
*about 2 tbsp fine dried white bread crumbs*

### PREPARATION

**1** Cut the steak and chicken into strips, and mix well with all the marinade ingredients. Let stand for at least 3 hours, but not longer than 12 hours.

**2** Make the peanut sauce: Heat the oil in a heavy-bottomed pan over medium-high heat and stir-fry the dry ingredients until browned. Stir in the lemon juice and chicken stock, and reduce slightly. Add sufficient bread crumbs to thicken. Allow to cool.

**3** Thread the steak and chicken strips separately onto about 25 x 5-in (12-cm) presoaked saté sticks. Broil for 2–3 minutes on each side, until brown. Serve hot, with the peanut sauce.

### SOAK & COOK

*It is important to marinate raw fish, meat, poultry, and sea food before it is broiled. The marinade not only adds flavor, it also has a tenderizing effect because of its acid content. Do not marinate fish in a lemon or lime marinade for more than 2 hours, or it will begin to "cook" in the acid.*

# TUNA & RED PEPPER KEBABS WITH GINGER-SOY MARINADE

*Seasoned with a pungent, Japanese style marinade, these delicate kebabs need no sauce, just a squeeze of lime or lemon if you like.*
*Makes about 25*

### INGREDIENTS

1/4 cup (60 ml) soy sauce
2 tbsp rice vinegar
2 tbsp canola or sunflower oil
2 tbsp water
1 tbsp dark sesame oil
1/4 tsp sugar
3 scallions, both white and green parts, finely chopped
2 garlic cloves, finely chopped or crushed
2 tbsp grated fresh ginger
2 tbsp finely chopped lemon grass
(1 lb) 500 g fresh tuna, cut into 1-in (2.5-cm) cubes
1 medium red pepper, cored, seeded, and cut into 1/2-in (1-cm) squares

### PREPARATION

1 Put the soy sauce, rice vinegar, canola or sunflower oil, water, sesame oil, and sugar in a large bowl, and whisk together. Add the scallions, garlic, ginger, and lemon grass, and combine well.
2 Add the tuna and toss together. Cover and marinate, in or out of the refrigerator, for 30 minutes, stirring occasionally. Stir in the red pepper after the first 15 minutes.
3 Thread the pieces of tuna and pepper onto about 25 presoaked small skewers, allowing 2 pieces of tuna to 1 piece of red pepper. Arrange the skewers on a baking sheet.
4 Place the baking sheet under a preheated broiler, 5–6 in (12–15 cm) from the heat. After 1 minute, turn the skewers over and baste the fish with the marinade. Cook another minute, and remove from the heat. The fish should be pink on the inside. Serve hot.

### Suggested Dipping Sauces

- *Quick Dipping Sauce (see page 88)*
- *Teriyaki Sauce (see page 94)*
- *Tahini-Tamari Sauce (see page 94)*

# MIDDLE EASTERN MEATBALLS

*Makes 100–120 small meatballs*

### INGREDIENTS

1 cup (175 g) fine bulgur wheat
1 large white onion, chopped
salt and freshly ground pepper
1 lb (500 g) ground lamb or beef
1/2–1 tsp ground cinnamon
1/2–1 tsp ground cumin
2 tbsp water
1/4 cup (35 g) sesame seeds, toasted
1 1/2 lb (750 g) zucchini, cut into 1/4-in (5-mm) slices and sautéed lightly
Tahini-Yogurt Dip (see page 29)

### PREPARATION

1 Soak the bulgur wheat for 15 minutes.
2 Meanwhile, place the onion with 1 tsp salt in a food processor fitted with the metal blade and blend to a coarse purée. Remove, and set aside.
3 Place the meat in the food processor and process until smooth and pasty. Add the onion and salt mixture, and cinnamon, cumin, and pepper to taste. Grind together until evenly mixed, then while the machine is running, add the water. The mixture should still be smooth and pasty.
4 Drain the bulgur wheat and squeeze out any excess water. Add to the meat mixture, and process again until smooth.
5 Moisten your hands and form the meat mixture into small balls, about ¾ in (2 cm) in diameter. The mixture will be sticky, but quite workable.
6 Place the meatballs on a baking sheet and broil, about 4–5 in (10–12 cm) from the heat, for 2½–3 minutes.
7 Spread the toasted sesame seeds on a board and roll the meatballs over them to coat. Serve threaded on toothpicks, with a slice of zucchini, and accompanied by the Tahini-Yogurt Dip or any dip of your choice (see left).

### VARIATION

SPICY MEATBALLS: Use *1 tsp ground cumin*, and add *1 tsp paprika* to the mixture. You could also add *ground allspice*, *more black pepper*, and *a few cloves of finely chopped garlic*.

# A Mexican Fiesta

*Create a festive mood with the vibrant flavors and vivid colors of these Mexican recipes. Spicy dips and toppings served with nacho chips or crunchy endive leaves are complemented by fresh and chocolate-coated fruit.*

**Chicken Nachos
with Salsa Verde
(page 83)**

*Seviche on endive
leaves (page 104)*

*Fresh Tomato Salsa (page 29) with nacho chips (page 81)*

*Mexican Fruit Platter (page 132)*

*Guacamole (page 83) with nacho chips*

# MARINATED FISH

Tartares and seviches make delicate hors d'oeuvres. Serve them on bread, pita crisps, crackers, or vegetable wafers – their fresh flavors go well with them. Seviche can also be served on endive leaves or on nacho chips.

★

## MUSSELS ON THE HALF SHELL

*This is a beautiful way to present mussels. First they are steamed, then tossed in a sauce, and finally, they are set back in their shells. The sauce you choose will determine the nature of the dish: if you choose a salsa, the dish will have a Mexican character; the other choices will have Mediterranean flavors.*
*Serves 10–12*

### INGREDIENTS

*2 quarts (1.5 kg) mussels*
*1/4 cup (60 ml) salt or vinegar*
*1 cup (250 ml) dry white wine*
*1 cup (250 ml) water*
*2 shallots or 1 onion, chopped*
*4 garlic cloves, crushed*
*2 1/2 cups (600 ml) Fresh Tomato Salsa (see page 29)*
*Tomato Concassée (see page 72), Basil Pesto (see page 25),*
*or Cilantro Pesto (see page 25)*
*cilantro, flat-leaf parsley, or basil for garnish (depending on which sauce you choose)*

### PREPARATION

**1** Brush the mussels and scrape off any barnacles; pull off the beards. Discard any with cracked shells, or those that do not close when tapped.
**2** Place in a bowl and rinse in several changes of cold water. Cover with cold water and stir in the salt or vinegar. Let stand for 15 minutes. Drain, rinse, and soak again for another 15 minutes. Drain and rinse again.
**3** Combine the wine, water, shallots or onion, and garlic in a large saucepan and bring to a boil. Add the mussels, cover, and steam for 5 minutes, shaking the pan or stirring halfway through to redistribute the mussels.

**4** Remove the pan from the heat and strain the cooking liquid through a cheesecloth-lined strainer into a bowl. Set aside.
**5** Remove the mussels from their shells, discarding any that have not opened, and set half the shells aside. Rinse the mussels quickly.
**6** In a large bowl, mix together the sauce of your choice with 1 cup (250 ml) of the strained cooking liquid from the mussels. Toss the mussels with this mixture, cover, and let marinate in the refrigerator for 1 hour or longer.
**7** To serve, place the mussels on the reserved shells and spoon on some sauce. Arrange on a platter and garnish with fresh herbs.

 *You cannot speed up cleaning the mussels, because each one of them must be inspected to make sure it closes when tapped. However, you can save time by buying prepared salsa, pesto, or tomato sauce for the marinade.*
*The cooked mussels can be refrigerated in the marinade for up to 24 hours.*

### VARIATION

**CLAMS ON THE HALF SHELL:** Substitute *1 quart (1.5 kg) clams* for the mussels.

—— *Fresh Fish* ——

*The most important thing to consider when you are serving raw or marinated fish is the quality of the fish itself.*
*Uncooked fish must be impeccably fresh. Buy from a reputable fish store, and only on the day you wish to serve it. To be extra sure, particularly about salmon, ask the fish seller if the fish has been fresh-frozen – parasites cannot survive in fish that has been frozen for 72 hours. Do not buy the fish unless you are absolutely sure of this.*

# FISH TARTARE

*Fish tartare is minced raw fish tossed with a sauce.*
*Here I use Horseradish Sauce, but you can also use any*
*of the others suggested below.*
*Serves 12–15*

## INGREDIENTS

*1 lb (500 g) center-cut tuna fillet, dark meat and*
*connective tissue removed,*
*or salmon fillet, skin and small bones removed*
*2 shallots, finely chopped*
*2 tbsp capers, drained and rinsed*
*1 ripe but firm avocado, peeled, pitted,*
*and diced very fine (optional)*
*1/4 cup (60 ml) lemon or lime juice*
*1 tsp Worcestershire sauce*
*salt and freshly ground pepper*

**FOR THE HORSERADISH SAUCE**

*3 tbsp grated fresh horseradish,*
*or 1 1/2–2 tbsp prepared horseradish*
*1/4 cup (60 ml) fromage blanc (see page 156) or sour cream*
*2 tbsp sherry vinegar*
*2 tbsp olive oil*
*2 tbsp water*
*1 tsp soy sauce*
*salt and freshly ground pepper*

**FOR SERVING**

*24 crostini (see page 69), pita triangles,*
*or thin slices of cucumber*
*chopped fresh herbs and herb sprigs, such as chives,*
*parsley, chervil, and dill*
*lemon or lime wedges*

## PREPARATION

1 Mince the fish in a food processor, or chop it very finely with a sharp knife. Do not purée. Toss with the shallots, capers, avocado (if using), lemon or lime juice, Worcestershire sauce, and salt and pepper to taste.

2 Make the Horseradish Sauce: Combine all the ingredients in a blender or whisk together in a bowl, until smooth.

3 Toss the fish in the sauce, cover, and let marinate in the refrigerator for about 1 1/2 hours.

4 To serve, either transfer to an attractive bowl and surround with crostini, pita triangles, or cucumber slices, or use as a topping for canapés. Garnish with chopped fresh herbs, herb sprigs, and lemon or lime wedges.

## VARIATIONS

Substitute the Horseradish Sauce with *Cilantro Pesto (see page 25), Asian Sesame-Ginger Dip (see page 29), or Mustard Sauce (see Gravadlax, page 104).*

# MARINATED RAW FISH ON TOOTHPICKS

*Small squares of marinated tuna or salmon may be served as mini-brochettes on toothpicks, as illustrated below. Sliced pickled ginger is available at Asian food shops.*
*Serves 10*

## INGREDIENTS

*1 lb (500 g) center-cut tuna fillet, dark meat and*
*connective tissue removed,*
*or salmon fillet, skin and small bones removed*
*salt and freshly ground pepper*
*1 tbsp soy sauce*
*1 tbsp rice vinegar or balsamic vinegar*
*2 tbsp mirin (Japanese sweet rice wine), or 2 tsp sugar*
*1-in (2.5-cm) piece of fresh ginger, grated*
*3 oz (90 g) pickled ginger*
*2 tsp water*
*4–5 scallions, white parts only,*
*sliced thickly on the diagonal*
*dipping sauce of your choice*

## PREPARATION

1 Cut the fish into 1/2-in (1-cm) cubes. Place in a bowl and toss with salt and pepper to taste.

2 Mix together the soy sauce, vinegar, mirin or sugar, fresh ginger, and water, and toss with the fish. Cover, and let marinate in the refrigerator for 30 minutes–1 hour.

3 Thread the fish, pickled ginger, and scallion slices on wooden toothpicks.

4 Serve with Horseradish Sauce (see Fish Tartare), Cilantro Pesto (see page 25), Asian Sesame-Ginger Dip (see page 29), or Mustard Sauce (see Gravadlax, page 104).

*Marinated Raw Fish*
*on Toothpicks with*
*Horseradish Sauce*

# SEVICHE

*Seviche is a Latin American dish of marinated raw fish. The fish, in fact, is no longer raw when you eat it, because the lime juice "cooks" it during marinating.*
*Serves 12–15*

## INGREDIENTS

*1 1/2 lb (750 g) very fresh fish fillets, such as cod, whiting, red snapper, or bream;*
*or the same weight center-cut tuna fillet, trimmed of dark meat and connective tissue;*
*or 1 1/2 lb (750 g) shelled scallops*
*1 1/2–2 cups (350–500 ml) lime juice (of about 7 large limes)*
*1 small onion, sliced*
*2 garlic cloves, finely chopped or crushed*
*1–2 fresh or canned jalapeño or serrano peppers, seeded and chopped*
*2 medium tomatoes, chopped*
*1 large or 2 small ripe avocados, peeled, pitted, and diced*
*2–4 tbsp olive oil*
*salt and freshly ground pepper*
*4–5 tbsp chopped cilantro*
*small lettuce or endive leaves, or 24 crostini (see page 69), or nacho chips (see page 81) for serving*

## PREPARATION

1 Cut the fish or scallops into 1/2-in (1-cm) cubes and place in a bowl. Pour on the lime juice and toss together well. Cover and refrigerate.

2 Marinate white fish or scallops for 7 hours, tossing every once in a while. Marinate tuna for about 1 1/2 hours or a little longer. It should remain pink in the middle.

3 Add the onion, garlic, peppers, tomatoes, and avocado. Then add olive oil, and salt and pepper to taste. Toss together, cover, and refrigerate for another hour.

4 Remove from the refrigerator, and stir in the cilantro, adding more to taste if you prefer. Adjust seasonings. Let stand for 15–30 minutes.

5 Before serving, place the seviche in a colander set over a bowl, and drain off most of the marinade.

6 Serve on small lettuce or endive leaves, or on crostini or nacho chips. If you prefer, you can serve all of the seviche on a platter or in a salad bowl, encircled by lettuce or endive leaves.

# GRAVADLAX

*The Scandinavian classic, gravadlax, sometimes also called gravlax, is sugar-and-salt-cured salmon. Although it needs 4 days to marinate, the results are worth it.*
*Serves 12–15*

## INGREDIENTS

*2 x 1 lb (500 g) center-cut salmon fillets, skin left on*
*3 tbsp coarse sea salt*
*3 tbsp sugar*
*2 tbsp vodka or aquavit*
*1 tbsp black peppercorns, crushed*
*1 1/2 cups (90 g) chopped fresh dill*
*cucumber slices and pumpernickel bread for serving*
*lemon or lime wedges and dill sprigs for garnish*
**FOR THE MUSTARD SAUCE**
*1/2 cup (125 ml) canola or sunflower oil*
*1/2 cup (125 ml) plain nonfat yogurt*
*1/4 cup (60 ml) coarse-grained mustard*
*1/4 cup (60 ml) lime juice*
*salt and freshly ground pepper*

## PREPARATION

1 Score each salmon fillet on the skin side, making several diagonal cuts about 1/8-in (3-mm) deep.

2 Combine the salt and sugar, and sprinkle 5 tsp over the bottom of a large glass or earthenware baking dish.

3 Place 1 salmon fillet, skin side down, in the dish. Sprinkle with half the vodka or aquavit, then sprinkle with the peppercorns. Sprinkle with 4 tsp of the salt and sugar mixture, and spread half the dill over the fillet in an even layer.

4 Rub 4 tsp of the salt and sugar mixture over the flesh side of the remaining fillet. Place this, skin side up, on top of the first fillet. Rub the remaining salt and sugar mixture over the top.

5 Cover the salmon with a sheet of waxed paper, then foil. Place a flat object, such as a chopping board, on top and weigh down with 3–5 lb (1.5–2.5 kg) cans of food, or weights.

6 Refrigerate for 48 hours. Check after 5–6 hours, and drain any liquid accumulated in the dish. Check again every 12 hours. Turn the salmon and refrigerate for another 48 hours, turning twice.

7 In the meantime, just before serving, make the Mustard Sauce: Whisk together all the ingredients, with salt and pepper to taste. Cover and refrigerate.

8 To serve the salmon, remove the skin, and cut the fish into very thin slices. Sprinkle with the remaining dill. Serve on cucumber slices or pieces of pumpernickel, with the Mustard Sauce, lemon or lime wedges, and dill sprigs.

**FISH ON A DISH**

*Translucent slices of delicate Gravadlax are served on cucumber slices and pieces of pumpernickel and garnished with Mustard Sauce, lemon or lime wedges, and dill sprigs. More Mustard Sauce is served alongside.*

# CARPACCIO

Carpaccio is paper-thin slices of raw beef, salmon, or tuna. It is often accompanied by a pungent sauce. It is delicious served on crostini (see page 69), pita bread, cheese crackers, or thin wafers of vegetables.

★

## BEEF CARPACCIO

*This is the classic carpaccio, dressed with olive oil and lemon and traditionally served with arugula leaves and shavings of Parmesan cheese (as illustrated on page 60).*
*Serves 8–10*

### INGREDIENTS

*3 x ¼-lb (125-g) pieces of beef filet mignon*
*¼ cup (60 ml) olive oil*
*¼ cup (60 ml) lemon juice*
*arugula leaves*
*18–24 crostini (see page 69)*
*salt and freshly ground pepper*
*18–24 Parmesan Shavings (see page 154) for garnish*

### PREPARATION

**1** Wrap each piece of beef in foil, and chill in the freezer for 1–2 hours, until just about to freeze.
**2** Whisk together the olive oil and lemon juice.
**3** Remove the beef from the freezer, unwrap, and slice paper-thin. Flatten the slices by pounding them between 2 pieces of waxed paper.
**4** Cut the slices into 1½-in (3.5-cm) pieces. Tear the arugula leaves into pieces and place a piece on each crostini. Top with a piece of beef and drizzle on a little of the olive oil and lemon dressing. Sprinkle with salt and pepper and garnish with the Parmesan Shavings.

### VARIATION

**BEEF CARPACCIO ROLLS:** Cut *¾ lb (375 g) Beef Carpaccio* into strips 1 in (2.5 cm) wide and 2 in (5 cm) long. Place *½–1 tsp Horseradish Sauce* at one end of each beef strip, or spread it evenly along the strip, and gently roll up the strip. Serve on *croutons, or daikon radish slices,* or spear the rolls with toothpicks.

────── *Sauces for Carpaccio* ──────

• *Cilantro Pesto (see page 25)*
• *Horseradish Sauce (see page 103)*
• *Asian Sesame-Ginger Dip (see page 29)*
• *Mustard Sauce (see page 104)*

## SALMON CARPACCIO

*Serves 8–10*

### INGREDIENTS

*1 lb (500 g) salmon fillet*
*sauce of your choice (see left)*
*18–24 crostini (see page 69)*
*salt and freshly ground pepper*

### PREPARATION

**1** Skin, wrap, and freeze the salmon as directed in steps 1 and 2 on page 107.
**2** Prepare your chosen sauce.
**3** Remove the salmon from the freezer and cut into slices as directed in step 3 on page 107.
**4** Spread each crostini with a little sauce, then top with pieces of salmon. Season to taste, arrange on a platter, and garnish as desired.

### VARIATIONS

**TUNA CARPACCIO:** Substitute *1 lb (500 g) center-cut tuna steak fillet, dark meat and connective tissue removed,* for the salmon.
**TUNA CARPACCIO ROLLS:** Cilantro Pesto (see page 25) goes very well with Tuna Carpaccio. Cut *1 lb (500 g) Tuna Carpaccio* into strips 1 in (2.5 cm) wide and 2 in (5 cm) long. Place *1 tsp Cilantro Pesto* at one end of each tuna strip, or spread it evenly along the strip, and gently roll up the strip. Serve on *croutons,* or *cucumber slices,* or spear the rolls with toothpicks.

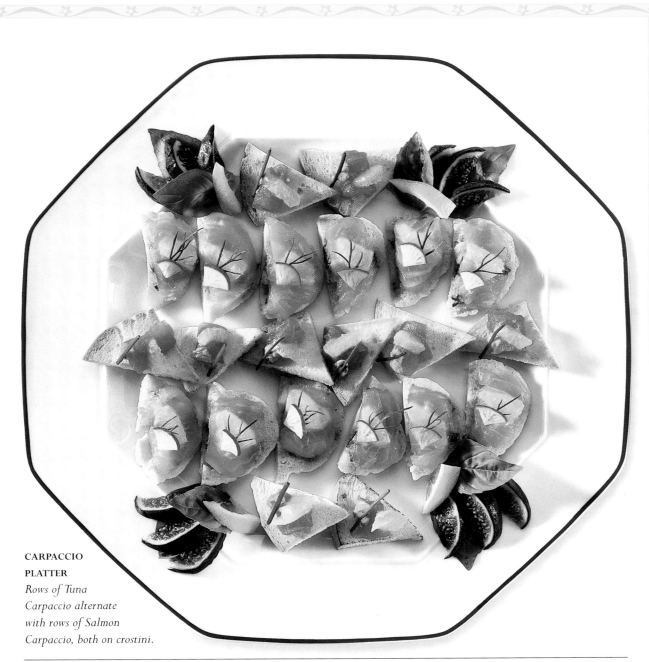

**CARPACCIO PLATTER**
*Rows of Tuna Carpaccio alternate with rows of Salmon Carpaccio, both on crostini.*

## PREPARING SALMON CARPACCIO

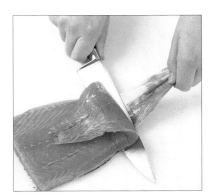

*1* Grasp the salmon skin at the tail end and, with a sawing action, work a sharp chef's knife between the skin and the flesh from the tail end.

*2* Roll and wrap the skinned salmon fillet tightly in foil. Chill in the freezer for 10–15 minutes, until just about to freeze.

*3* Unwrap the chilled salmon and slice as thinly as possible. Squeeze the slices between waxed paper with your fingers, and cut to fit the crostini.

# PATES & TERRINES

Traditionally served as hors d'oeuvres, pâtés and terrines may be some of the most elaborate and time-consuming recipes to prepare, but they are well worth the extra effort and attention. Their rich, meaty textures and flavors add substance to a party spread and you will find that a little goes a long way. Rather than serving my terrines whole, I prefer to cut them into dainty slices and serve them on different-shaped canapés, while I spread the pâtés on tiny canapés and garnish them prettily to make them as appealing as possible.

**MEATY CANAPES**

*Mounds of rich Brandied Liver Pâté (right) on triangular canapés are garnished with slices of gherkin, a dab of sun-dried tomato paste, and parsley.*

*Brandied Liver Pâté*

*Duck Terrine*

**POTTED DUCK**

*Slices of Duck Terrine (above) are served on floral-shaped canapés. They are garnished with fans made from slices of gherkin cut lengthwise and topped with a dab of sun-dried tomato paste and parsley.*

*Brandied Liver Pâté*

## To Make Pate & Terrine Canapes

**1** Cut thick slices of bread into an assortment of attractive shapes with pastry cutters. Toast until light golden on both sides.

**2** Cut thin slices from terrines and cut the slices with a pastry cutter or into smaller slices to fit the canapés. Alternatively, set terrines in ramekins or other small molds, unmold, and cut slices lengthwise.

**3** Arrange the slices of terrine on the canapés and garnish as desired.

**4** For Brandied Liver Pâté canapés, simply spread the pâté, smooth into a neat shape, and garnish as desired.

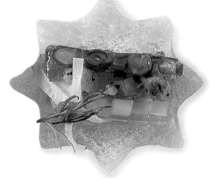

*Duck Terrine*

**SEE-THROUGH SLICES**

*Star-shaped canapés make a delicate base for slices of Lamb Terrine en Gelée, the colorful ingredients showing through the light jelly (right). A dab of sun-dried tomato paste and a sprig of dill top the garnish of crossed blanched turnip sticks.*

*Lamb Terrine en Gelée*

# PATES & TERRINES

*Pâtés are a smooth mixture of finely ground meat, often set with butter. They can be served sliced or spread on canapés. Terrines are more elaborate: different meats or vegetables are layered either with a mixture of ground meat or a meat or poultry jelly. To appreciate their intricate layers, serve them sliced.*

★

## BRANDIED LIVER PATE

*This is a luxurious-tasting pâté that is extremely quick and simple to put together with the help of a food processor.*
*Serves 10*

### INGREDIENTS

*6 tbsp (90 g) butter*
*1 large shallot, sliced*
*1 lb (500 g) chicken livers*
*1/2 tsp salt*
*5 whole black peppercorns*
*2 tsp fresh thyme leaves, or 1 tsp dried thyme*
*3 tbsp cognac (or Madeira, sherry, or Armagnac)*

### PREPARATION

**1** Melt half the butter over medium-high heat in a frying pan and add the shallot. Fry gently, stirring, for about 1 minute.

**2** Add the chicken livers. Cook, stirring, until the centers of the livers are faintly pink. Do not allow the livers or the shallots to brown. Remove from the heat and let the livers cool in the juices in the pan.

**3** Transfer the contents of the pan, including the pan juices, to a food processor fitted with the metal blade. Add the salt, peppercorns, and thyme, and purée until smooth.

**4** With the machine running, add the cognac, then the remaining butter, a little at a time. Continue to purée until the mixture is smooth.

**5** Transfer to a ramekin or other serving dish. Cover well and chill. The pâté should have the spreading consistency of semi-firm butter. Bring to room temperature before serving.

 *The pâté will keep for 5 days in the refrigerator. Bring to room temperature before serving.*

## DUCK TERRINE

*Start making this terrine well in advance. You will need a day for marinating the meat (during which time you should make the stock for the demi-glace), and the cooked terrine should sit in the refrigerator for 3–5 days or even up to a week before serving, to allow the flavors to ripen.*
*Serves 15–20*

### INGREDIENTS

**FOR THE TERRINE**
*1 1/2 medium ducks to yield:*
*2 whole duck breasts, total weight 1/2 lb (250 g)*
*and 2 lb (1 kg) boned duck meat (not breast meat),*
*skin, fat, and tendons removed, cut into 3/4-in (2-cm) cubes*
*1 lb (500 g) chicken livers*
*3/4 lb (375 g) fresh pork belly fat, diced*
*2 x 1-in (2.5-cm) pieces of orange peel*
*3 tbsp whole coriander seeds, ground*
*1 1/2–2 tbsp salt*
*1 tbsp sugar*
*2 tsp dried thyme*
*2–2 1/2 tsp freshly ground pepper*
*1 tsp grated fresh ginger*
*3/4 tsp ground cinnamon*
*1/2 tsp ground cloves*
*1/2 tsp ground bay leaves*
*2 pinches of freshly grated nutmeg*
*6 tbsp (90 ml) dry white wine*
*1/2 cup (125 ml) cognac*
*2 tbsp (30 g) butter or duck fat (from the underside of the duck skin)*
*3 oz (90 g) shallots, finely chopped (to make 1/4 cup/60 ml when cooked)*
*2 tbsp (15 g) cornstarch*
*1/2 cup (125 ml) crème fraîche or heavy cream*
*1 garlic clove, finely chopped or crushed*
*2 eggs, beaten*
*3/4 cup (175 ml) duck demi-glace (see page 111)*
*2 1/2 oz (75 g) pork caul,*
*or 1/2 lb (250 g) thinly sliced fresh pork fat,*
*for lining the terrine*
*1/2 cup (60 g) shelled and skinned pistachios (optional)*

**FOR THE STOCK AND DEMI-GLACE**

*1 1/2 tbsp butter*
*1 duck carcass, cut up*
*2 medium carrots, chopped*
*1 medium onion, quartered*
*3 quarts (3 liters) water, or to cover*
*2 x 1-in (2·5-cm) slices of orange peel*
*1/2-in (1-cm) piece of fresh ginger,*
*peeled and thinly sliced*
*1 bouquet garni, made with 3 sprigs each of parsley and*
*cilantro, 2 bay leaves, and 2 sprigs of fresh thyme*
*1/4-in (5-mm) piece of cinnamon stick*
*1/2 piece of star anise*
*1 tsp salt*
*1 tsp peppercorns*
*1/2 tsp Szechwan pepper*

## PREPARATION

### THE FIRST DAY

1 Wrap the whole duck breasts in waxed paper and refrigerate.

2 Combine the remaining duck meat with the chicken livers and pork fat. Add the orange peel, coriander, salt, sugar, thyme, pepper, ginger, cinnamon, cloves, bay, and nutmeg.

3 Heat the wine briefly in a saucepan, remove from the heat, and set alight. When the flames die down, cool and stir into the meat mixture, with the cognac. Mix, cover, and refrigerate for 24 hours. Stir often to distribute the flavors.

4 Meanwhile, make the stock, which will be reduced for the demi-glace: Melt the butter in a large, heavy-bottomed saucepan over medium heat and brown the cut-up duck carcass, carrots, and onion, stirring constantly.

5 Add the water and the remaining ingredients and bring to a simmer. Skim the surface. Cover, reduce the heat, and simmer for 2 hours, skimming from time to time, until the stock is richly flavored, but not too salty. Strain through a cheesecloth-lined strainer.

6 Return the stock to the saucepan, bring to a boil, and reduce to 3/4 cup (175 ml). Remove the demi-glace from the heat and let cool. Refrigerate overnight.

### THE NEXT DAY

7 Grind the meat mixture twice, in small batches, through the large cutting grill of a meat grinder, or in a food processor fitted with the metal blade, using the pulse action.

8 Melt 1 tbsp butter or duck fat in a small skillet over medium-low heat. Add the shallots, and cook, stirring, for about 5 minutes, until tender. Stir into the meat mixture, with the cornstarch, crème fraîche or cream, garlic, eggs, and the demi-glace.

9 Cut the duck breasts lengthwise into strips 1/2 in (1 cm) wide. Season lightly with salt and pepper. Melt the remaining 1 tbsp butter or duck fat in a heavy-bottomed skillet over medium-high heat. Brown the strips on all sides for about 5 minutes. They should be cooked through but slightly pink.

10 Line a heavy, lidded 1 1/2-quart (1.5-liter) terrine mold with the pork caul or slices of pork fat, leaving enough overhanging to cover the top of the terrine. If the pieces are not large enough for this, set aside a sufficient quantity to cover the top of the terrine later.

11 Fill with one-quarter of the meat mixture. If using pistachios, sprinkle in half of them in an even layer. Cover with a quarter of the meat mixture. Lay strips of duck breast lengthwise over the meat mixture in a single layer. Cover with a quarter of the meat mixture. Sprinkle on the remaining pistachios, and lay any remaining strips of duck breast on top.

12 Cover with the remaining meat mixture (don't worry if the meat goes over the rim, it will reduce in volume as it cooks). Fold the overhanging caul or pork fat over the terrine, and cover tightly with the lid.

13 Tap the mold squarely on the work surface once, to get rid of any air pockets. Place in a baking pan and fill with water. Place in the lower half of a 325°F (160°C) oven, and bake for 2–2 1/2 hours, until a meat thermometer reads 160°F (70°C) when inserted three-quarters of the way down in the middle. Let cool, then refrigerate for 3–7 days before serving.

# LAMB TERRINE EN GELEE

*This is a light, simple terrine that is very attractive when unmolded, because the ingredients show through the gelée or jelly that holds them together. Slices are even prettier, with the colorful pieces of the vegetables showing through.*

*Serves 12*

## INGREDIENTS

### FOR THE GELEE

*1 lb (500 g) lamb bones*
*2 medium carrots, coarsely chopped*
*1 large leek, cleaned and coarsely chopped*
*4 sprigs of basil or chervil*
*4 sprigs of flat-leaf parsley*
*3 bay leaves*
*2 cloves*
*1 tbsp coriander seeds*
*1 tbsp peppercorns*
*3 pints (1.5 liters) water*
*1¹/₂ tbsp gelatin powder*
*salt and freshly ground pepper*

### FOR THE TERRINE

*2 tbsp (30g) butter*
*3 medium carrots, cut into ¹/₄-in (5-mm) dice*
*1³/₄ lb (875 g) lamb, cut into ¹/₂-in (1-cm) dice*
*1 large bouquet of basil or chervil sprigs*
*(whichever used for the gelée)*
*5 oz (150 g) green beans, trimmed*
*2 medium turnips, peeled*
*and cut into ¹/₄-in (5-mm) thick strips*
*1 small red pepper, cored, seeded,*
*and finely diced*
*1 oz (30 g) fresh basil or chervil*
*(whichever used for the gelée), chopped*

## PREPARATION

1 Make the gelée: Combine all the ingredients, except for the gelatin and salt and pepper, in a large saucepan, and bring to a boil. Skim the surface with a large spoon to remove any froth. Cover, and cook over medium heat for 2 hours or longer, skimming occasionally, until you have a rich, aromatic broth.

2 Strain into a bowl through a cheesecloth-lined strainer and return the broth to the pan. Bring to a boil, and simmer until the broth is reduced to 1¹/₄ pints (750 ml).

3 Bring the broth to a boil again and stir in the gelatin powder until it dissolves. Remove from the heat. Add salt and pepper to taste (the cold gelée requires plenty of seasoning for the flavors to emerge).

4 In the meantime, while the broth is cooking, prepare the ingredients for the terrine: Melt half the butter over low heat in a flameproof casserole and add the carrots. Cook for 10 minutes, stirring occasionally. Add the remaining butter and the lamb, and cook, stirring, until the lamb has browned. Add the herb bouquet.

5 Cover, and place in a 300°F (150°C) oven for 2 hours, stirring every 15 minutes. Remove from the oven, and reduce any remaining liquid. Season with salt and pepper. Remove the herb bouquet.

6 Bring a large pan of water to a boil. Add 1 tsp salt, and the green beans. Cook for 5 minutes, until tender. Remove from the pan with a slotted spoon and refresh under cold water. Add the turnips to the boiling water and cook for 5–10 minutes, until tender. Drain and refresh under cold water. Set aside.

7 If the gelée has set, heat gently to liquefy. Stir in the red pepper. Add half the herbs to the gelée and half to the meat mixture. Spoon enough gelée into a 1-quart (1-liter) terrine mold to cover the bottom by ¹/₂ in (1 cm). Place in the freezer for a few minutes to set.

8 Remove the mold from the freezer and add a layer of half the meat mixture. Pour on enough gelée to cover. Place in the freezer again for a few minutes to set.

9 Remove the mold from the freezer and add a layer of green beans. Cover with gelée, and place in the freezer again for a few minutes.

10 Repeat with the turnips and the remaining meat, ending with a layer of gelée. (You can also arrange the meat and vegetables in several alternating layers if you wish, pouring on gelée to cover each layer.)

11 Cover the mold and place in the refrigerator for at least 3 hours, or until set.

12 To unmold, run a sharp knife between the edges of the terrine and the mold, then dip the mold in hot water for no more than 1 minute, to loosen the gelée. Invert a plate or platter over the top of the terrine, and flip over. If the terrine does not unmold, dip again briefly in hot water: be careful not to immerse for too long, or the gelée at the sides will melt and destroy the shape of the terrine.

# DESSERTS

*A selection of desserts is the climax of any party — and they always looks colorful. A fresh fruit platter served with creamy dips, or petits fours, might be all that is necessary. On the other hand, you might want to offer cakes and pastries together with fruit. The fruit tartlets or the choux puffs filled with coffee cream are always sensational, while chocolate-coated fruit and chocolate bouchées will provide a luxurious finishing touch to any meal.*

# DESSERT TARTLETS

Bite-sized tartlets are easy to make and the basic tartlet shell is extremely versatile. You can serve prebaked and cooled pastry shells filled with a choice of fruit on a bed of Crème Pâtissière (see page 153) or cream cheese as shown here. For baked tartlets, fill partially baked pastry shells from the choice of fillings given on pages 116–119, and bake through.

## FRESH FRUIT TARTLETS

*Makes 16 x 2-in (5-cm) tartlets*
*or 10 x 3-in (7-cm) tartlets*

### INGREDIENTS

*¹/₂ lb (250 g) cream cheese*
*2 tbsp plain nonfat yogurt*
*2 tbsp sugar*
*2 tsp finely grated lemon zest*
*2 tsp lemon juice*
*16 x 2-in (5-cm) or 10 x 3-in (7-cm) tartlet shells made*
*with Almond Dessert Pastry, baked and cooled*
*(see pages 140–141)*
*mixed fresh fruit of your choice (see below)*
*1 cup (200 g) apricot jam*

### PREPARATION

**1** In a food processor fitted with the metal blade, blend together the cream cheese, yogurt, sugar, lemon zest, and lemon juice.

**2** Spoon the cream-cheese mixture into the tartlet shells.

**3** Arrange the fruit of your choice decoratively on top of the cream-cheese filling, cutting them into halves, quarters, or slices to fit as necessary.

**4** Melt the jam in a saucepan. Press through a strainer, then quickly brush over the fruit while the glaze is still warm, taking care not to disturb your arrangement.

**A CORNUCOPIA OF FRUIT**
*A selection of fresh fruit to fill tartlets can include raspberries, blueberries, strawberries, clementines, mandarin oranges, cherries, figs, kiwi fruit, and mangoes.*

*Fresh Fruit Tartlets*

# BAKED TARTLETS

The fillings in these tartlets are baked in their pastry shells. Use unbaked or partially baked Pâte Sucrée or Almond Dessert Pastry (see pages 140–141), or Rough Puff Pastry (see page 139) for the shells. Instead of making individual tartlets, you can also make a large 10-in (25-cm) tart.

★

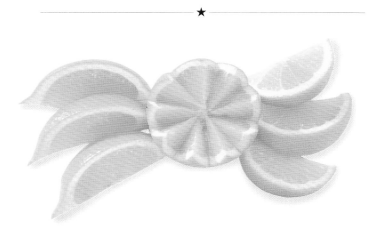

## LEMON TARTLETS

*Makes 24 x 2-in (5-cm) or 16 x 3-in (7-cm) tartlets*

### INGREDIENTS

*2/3 cup (165 ml) lemon juice*
*1/2 cup (125 g) sugar*
*2 tbsp plain nonfat yogurt or crème fraîche*
*4 eggs*
*24 x 2-in (5-cm) or 16 x 3-in (7-cm) tartlet shells,*
*baked blind and cooled (see pages 139–141)*

### PREPARATION

**1** Whisk together the lemon juice and sugar. Add the yogurt or crème fraîche and combine well.
**2** Beat the eggs into the mixture, 1 at a time.
**3** Pour the custard mixture into the tartlet shells. Bake tartlets in a 375°F (190°C) oven for about 15 minutes or until the custard has set.

### VARIATION

**LIME TARTLETS:** Substitute *2/3 cup (165 ml) lime juice* for the lemon juice and *2 tbsp sour cream* for the crème fraîche.

## RHUBARB & HONEY TARTLETS

*Makes 24 x 2-in (5-cm) or 16 x 3-in (7-cm) tartlets*

### INGREDIENTS

*1 lb (500 g) rhubarb, cut into 1/2-in (1-cm) pieces*
*1/4 cup (60 ml) mild honey, such as lavender, acacia, or clover*
*1–2 tbsp sugar*
*1 tbsp Grand Marnier (optional)*
*24 x 2-in (5-cm) or 16 x 3-in (7-cm) unbaked tartlet shells*
*(see pages 139–141)*
*whipped cream for decoration*
*strawberries, halved lengthwise, for decoration (optional)*

### PREPARATION

**1** Combine the rhubarb, honey, and 1 tbsp sugar in a noncorrosive saucepan and bring to a boil over medium heat. Reduce the heat to medium-low, cover, and simmer for 10 minutes, stirring occasionally, until the rhubarb is tender.
**2** Increase the heat and cook for 10–15 minutes, stirring, until the mixture holds its shape.
**3** Let cool, then taste, and add more sugar, if you like. Stir in the Grand Marnier, if using.
**4** Spoon the mixture into the tartlet shells, and bake in a 400°F (200°C) oven for 10 minutes. Reduce the heat to 350°F (180°C) and bake tartlets for 10 minutes more.
**5** Let cool, and decorate with piped whipped cream and strawberry halves.

*Rhubarb & Honey
Tartlets in Rough Puff
Pastry shells*

## Using Rhubarb

*Rhubarb is a vegetable, but because it is extremely sour, it is sweetened considerably when cooked and therefore treated as a fruit. It makes a delicious partner for pastry and is often served with other fruit, especially oranges and strawberries.*

*Rhubarb must be handled cautiously. Its leaves contain oxalic acid and can be poisonous: always discard them before cooking.*

*Take care while cooking rhubarb as it tends to sputter. To avoid being burned, use a long-handled spoon.*

*To test if the cooked rhubarb will set for Rhubarb & Honey Tartlets, pour a little of the mixture onto a plate that has been chilled in the freezer for about 10 minutes. The rhubarb should hold its shape and not spread over the plate.*

**Rhubarb stems**

# RICH PECAN SQUARES

*Here, a pecan tart is baked in a rectangular pan,*
*then cut into small squares.*
*Makes 1 x 10- x 12-in (25- x 30-cm) tart*

## INGREDIENTS

*1 x 10- x 12-in (25- x 30-cm) unbaked tart shell made*
*with Pâte Sucrée (see pages 140–141)*
*4 tbsp (60 g) unsalted butter*
*1/2 cup (125 ml) mild honey*
*3 large eggs*
*1 tbsp rum*
*1 tsp vanilla extract (see page 156)*
*1/2 tsp salt*
*1/4 tsp freshly grated nutmeg*
*2 cups (250 g) broken pecans*

## PREPARATION

1 Partially bake the tart shell in a 375°F (190°C) oven for 5 minutes.
2 Cream the butter with the honey. Beat the eggs into the butter and honey mixture, 1 at a time.
3 Stir in the rum, vanilla extract, salt, and nutmeg. Fold in the pecans.
4 Pour the mixture into the partially baked shell, and bake in a 375°F (190°C) oven for 35–40 minutes, until a knife inserted in the center comes out clean.
5 Remove from the oven and let cool. Cut into 1½–2-in (3.5–5-cm) squares.

## VARIATION

**WALNUT SQUARES:** Substitute *maple syrup* for the honey, *cognac* for the rum, and *chopped walnuts* for the pecans.

**Rich Pecan Squares**

# APRICOT & ALMOND TARTLETS

*Makes 24 x 2-in (5-cm) or 16 x 3-in (7-cm) tartlets*

## INGREDIENTS

*1 cup (250 g) dried apricots*
*1 cup (150 g) blanched, skinned almonds, finely chopped*
*1/4 tsp almond extract (see page 156)*
*24 x 2-in (5-cm) or 16 x 3-in (7-cm) partially baked*
*tartlet shells (see page 139–141)*

## PREPARATION

1 Place the apricots in a bowl and pour on boiling water to cover. Let stand for 1 hour or longer.
2 Drain the apricots, and, if you like, dice into 1/4-in (5-mm) pieces. Place in a bowl and add the almonds and almond extract and mix together.
3 Divide the filling evenly among the partially baked tartlet shells and bake in a 400°F (200°C) oven for 15–20 minutes.

# MINCEMEAT TARTLETS

*Makes 36 x 2-in (5-cm) tartlets*

## INGREDIENTS

*1 seedless orange, including peel, cut into pieces*
*finely grated zest of lemon*
*1/2 cup (125 ml) apple juice*
*2 large tart apples, peeled and finely diced*
*1 cup (175 g) raisins*
*1/2 cup (90 g) chopped dates*
*1/2 cup (125 g) brown sugar*
*1/4 tsp ground cinnamon*
*1/4 tsp ground cloves*
*1/4 tsp freshly grated nutmeg*
*1/8 tsp salt*
*2 tbsp rum*
*1/4 tsp vanilla extract (see page 156)*
*36 x 2-in (5-cm) partially baked tartlet shells*
*(see pages 139–141)*

## PREPARATION

1 Blend the orange, lemon zest, and apple juice to a purée in a food processor fitted with the metal blade. Heat in a noncorrosive pan over a low heat. Stir in the apples, raisins, dates, sugar, spices, and salt. Cover and simmer for about 15 minutes, stirring occasionally. Remove from the heat and stir in the rum and vanilla.
2 Divide the filling evenly among the partially baked tartlet shells and bake in a 375°F (190°C) oven for 20 minutes.

# CHERRY CLAFOUTIS TARTLETS

*Makes 24 x 2-in (5-cm) or 16 x 3-in (7-cm) tartlets*

### INGREDIENTS

*1¹/₂ lb (750 g) fresh cherries, stems and pits removed*
*3 tbsp kirsch*
*6 tbsp (90 g) sugar*
*3 large eggs*
*1 vanilla bean, or ¹/₂ tsp vanilla extract (see page 156)*
*²/₃ cup (90 g) all-purpose flour, sifted*
*³/₄ cup (175 ml) plain nonfat yogurt*
*pinch of salt*
*24 x 2-in (5-cm) or 16 x 3-in (7-cm) partially baked*
*tartlet shells (see pages 139–141)*

### PREPARATION

**1** Toss the cherries with the kirsch and 2 tbsp of the sugar in a bowl. Let stand for 30 minutes.

**2** Drain the liquid from the cherries and beat together with the eggs, the seeds from the vanilla bean, or the vanilla extract, and the remaining sugar.

**3** Slowly beat in the flour. Add the yogurt and salt. Mix together well.

**4** Arrange a few cherries in each partially baked tartlet shell. Pour in the batter.

**5** Bake in a 400°F (200°C) oven for 25 minutes, or until the tops are browned and the filling firm. Cool on racks.

 *The tartlets will keep for several hours at room temperature.*

### VARIATIONS

**APRICOT CLAFOUTIS TARTLETS:** Substitute *apricots — blanched, peeled, halved and pitted* — for the cherries. You can use *canned apricots in syrup* in winter. Place one apricot half in each shell, either unsliced or sliced down to the base and fanned out. Pour on the batter and bake as above.

**GRAPE CLAFOUTIS TARTLETS:** Substitute *seedless grapes* for the cherries. Place as many as will fit in each tartlet shell, pour on the batter, and bake as above.

**BLACKBERRY OR RASPBERRY CLAFOUTIS TARTLETS:** Substitute *blackberries* or *raspberries* for the cherries. Place as many as will fit in each tartlet shell, pour on the batter, and bake as above.

**BLUEBERRY OR RED CURRANT CLAFOUTIS TARTLETS:** Substitute *blueberries* or *red currants* for the cherries. Place as many as will fit in each tartlet shell, pour on the batter, and bake as above.

# CRANBERRY-PEAR TARTLETS

*These are beautiful holiday tartlets: a festive fan of sliced pears around cranberry purée.*
*Makes 24 x 2-in (5-cm) or 16 x 3-in (7-cm) tartlets*

### INGREDIENTS

*³/₄ cup (175 ml) orange juice*
*2 tbsp cornstarch*
*¹/₂ cup (125 g) sugar*
*2¹/₂ cups (300 g) cranberries*
*2 tbsp finely grated orange zest*
*3 large comice pears, peeled, cored, and thinly sliced*
*(cut slices to fit the size of the tartlet shells if*
*they are too large)*
*2 tbsp lemon juice*
*24 x 2-in (5-cm) or 16 x 3-in (7-cm) partially baked*
*tartlet shells (see pages 139–141)*
*2 tbsp apricot jam*

### PREPARATION

**1** Combine the orange juice, cornstarch, and all but 2 tbsp of the sugar in a large saucepan. Add half the cranberries and bring to a boil, stirring. Remove from the heat and stir in the remaining cranberries and the orange zest. The mixture should be quite thick. Set aside.

**2** Toss the pear slices in a bowl with the remaining sugar and the lemon juice. Arrange them overlapping in a circle in the partially baked tartlet shells, reserving any juice. Place 1 tbsp of the cranberry sauce on top. Bake in a 400°F (200°C) oven for 20 minutes.

**3** Meanwhile, make a glaze: Melt the jam in a saucepan with any reserved pear juice.

**4** Remove the tartlets from the oven and brush with the glaze. Cool on racks before serving.

### VARIATION

**CHOCOLATE PEAR TARTLETS:** Chop *4 oz (125 g) semisweet chocolate*, and divide evenly between the tartlet shells. Whisk together *1 egg* with *²/₃ cup (150 ml) light cream*. Add *1-in (2.5-cm) piece of fresh ginger, chopped finely*. Pour over the chocolate in the tartlet shells. Peel, core, and slice *2 pears*, and arrange in the shells. Bake in a 400°F (200°C) oven for 20 minutes.

# CHOUX PUFFS

These feathery puffs can be filled simply with Crème Pâtissière (see recipe on page 153), with a coffee-flavored filling (see below), or with fresh fruit and Chantilly cream as illustrated here. Unfilled choux puffs freeze well. To thaw and crisp, transfer them from the freezer to a 425°F (220°C) oven and bake for about 4 minutes.

★

## COFFEE CREAM PUFFS

*Makes 40 puffs*

### INGREDIENTS

*1 cup (250 ml) milk*
*1 1/2 tbsp ground coffee*
*3 egg yolks*
*5 tbsp (75 g) superfine sugar*
*4 tbsp all-purpose flour, sifted*
*a little chilled butter*
*3/4 cup (175 ml) whipping cream*
*2 tbsp confectioners' sugar (or icing sugar)*
*40 choux puffs (see page 138), baked and cooled*

### PREPARATION

1 Scald the milk. Add the coffee and steep for 20 minutes or longer. Strain the mixture through a double layer of cheesecloth.

2 Beat the egg yolks and sugar together until thick and lemon-colored. Beat in the flour.

3 Slowly add the flavored milk to the egg yolk mixture, whisking constantly. Transfer to a heavy-bottomed saucepan and stir with a whisk or wooden spoon over medium heat, until the mixture thickens. Pour into a bowl.

4 Rub the surface of the coffee cream lightly with a piece of chilled butter, or place a piece of waxed paper directly over the surface, so that the cream does not form a skin. Let cool.

5 Whip the cream with 1 tbsp confectioners' sugar (or icing sugar) until stiff peaks form. Add 2 tbsp of the whipped cream to the coffee cream and whisk together well to lighten the mixture. Fold in the remaining whipped cream.

6 Remove the tops of the choux puffs and fill the bottoms with the coffee cream, as directed in steps 1 and 2 on page 121. Dust the lids lightly with the remaining confectioners' sugar (or icing sugar) and replace on the choux puffs.

## FRESH FRUIT & CREAM PUFFS

*Fresh fruit is tucked into a bed of Chantilly cream in the filling for these choux puffs. To enrich the Chantilly cream, add a flavoring to the whipped cream with the confectioners' sugar (or icing sugar). Vanilla, cognac, rum, or a liqueur are all good choices.*
*Makes 40 puffs*

### INGREDIENTS

*2 1/2 cups (600 ml) whipping cream*
*3–4 tbsp confectioners' sugar (or icing sugar)*
*40 choux puffs (see page 138), baked and cooled*
*1/2 lb (250 g) apricots, halved, pitted, and thinly sliced*
*3 kiwi fruit, peeled and sliced*
*7 oz (200 g) wild strawberries*
*7 oz (200 g) blueberries*
*mint leaves for decoration*

### PREPARATION

1 To make the Chantilly cream, pour the whipping cream into a chilled bowl and whip with a whisk or electric mixer until soft peaks form. Add 3 tbsp sugar, and whip until the cream forms soft peaks again and just holds its shape.

2 Remove the tops of the choux puffs and fill the bottoms with the Chantilly cream and fruit, as directed on page 121. Dust the lids lightly with sugar, replace on the choux puffs, and decorate with mint leaves.

### WILD & WONDERFUL

*Wild strawberries, also called alpine strawberries and fraises des bois, are renowned for their aroma, reminiscent of roses. The small, dark red berries grow to about 1/2 in (1 cm) long and do not need to be hulled. European varieties of cultivated strawberries are all derived from fraises des bois, but none equal their tantalizing flavor.*

**DAINTY CHOUX**
*Bite-sized Fresh Fruit &
Cream Puffs are decorated with
fresh mint leaves, with strawberry
leaves on the platter.*

## FILLING CHOUX PUFFS WITH CREAM & FRUIT

*1 Using a sharp knife, carefully cut
off the top from each choux puff
and reserve to use as lids.*

*2 Fill a pastry bag fitted with a star
tube with Chantilly cream, and pipe
into the bottoms of the puffs.*

*3 Gently press pieces of the prepared
fruit into the Chantilly cream to
make an attractive pattern on each puff.*

# CHOCOLATE DESSERTS

Few can resist chocolate – for many, it is the ultimate confection. Make your own delectable end-of-party collection from brownies, chocolate-coated fruit, and chocolate bouchées. Buy the best quality chocolate you can. The richest chocolate contains the highest percentage of cocoa solids: look for more than 60 percent.

*Chocolate-coated Fruit*

*Celebration Brownies*

**PARTY HIGHLIGHTS**

*Crown a party with chocolate desserts such as Chocolate-coated Fruit, Celebration Brownies, and chocolate bouchées.*

*White Chocolate
& Orange Bouchées*

## TO USE MELTED CHOCOLATE IN CHOCOLATE DESSERTS

- Dip fruit in melted chocolate (see page 124).

- Pipe melted chocolate onto Celebration Brownies (see page 124).

- Combine melted chocolate with whipped cream to fill chocolate shapes (see Dark Chocolate Bouchées, page 125).

*Dark Chocolate
Bouchées*

*Coffee & Nut Bouchées*

*Mocha Bouchées*

# CELEBRATION BROWNIES

*These moist, chewy cakelike cookies are usually made with chocolate, but can include butterscotch and vanilla. They are perfect, when decorated, for special occasions. Brownies should be soft inside and crisp outside. Do not overbake them or they will be too dry.*
*Makes 25–30*

## INGREDIENTS

*5 oz (150 g) bittersweet chocolate, broken into small pieces*
*1/4 cup (60 g) unsalted butter, more for greasing*
*1 1/4 cups (150 g) all-purpose flour, more for dusting*
*1/2 tsp baking powder*
*1/2 tsp salt*
*1/2 cup (125 g) superfine sugar*
*2 large eggs*
*3/4 cup (90 g) walnuts, shelled and chopped*
*2 oz (60 g) white chocolate for decoration (optional)*

## PREPARATION

1 Butter an 8-in (20-cm) square baking pan. Line it with waxed paper, butter the paper, and dust with flour.

2 Melt the bittersweet chocolate and butter together in a bowl set over a pan of simmering water, stirring every 15 seconds. Remove from the heat just before fully melted and stir to complete the melting. Let cool to room temperature.

3 Sift the flour, baking powder, and salt into a bowl.

4 Beat the sugar and eggs together in another bowl until pale and thick. Stir in the flour mixture, melted chocolate, and chopped nuts, and combine well.

5 Transfer the batter to the prepared baking pan, and bake in a 350°F (180°C) oven for 20–30 minutes, or until a toothpick inserted in the center comes out with just a little batter on it. The brownies should still be moist in the center when they are done.

6 Loosen the edges with a spatula. Invert the pan onto a baking sheet, remove the pan and the lining paper. Place another baking sheet that has been lightly greased over the brownies, then invert again and remove the top baking sheet. Let cool, then cut the brownies into small squares that are no more than 2 in (5 cm) square.

7 Melt the white chocolate, pour into a paper pastry bag (see page 151), and pipe a decorative pattern on top of each brownie.

# CHOCOLATE-COATED FRUIT

*Almost any fruit can be dipped in chocolate and served as a dessert, or you can serve a large platter of fruit around a fondue pot of melted chocolate. Supply toothpicks to dip the fruit in the chocolate.*
*Makes about 50*

## INGREDIENTS

*1 red apple*
*1 papaya*
*1/4 lb (125 g) cape gooseberries*
*1/4 lb (125 g) seedless green grapes*
*1/4 lb (125 g) bittersweet chocolate, broken into small pieces*

## PREPARATION

1 Core the apple and cut it into about 12 wedges. Peel and halve the papaya, remove the seeds, and cut the flesh into about 15 wedges, depending on the size of the fruit.

2 Dry the cut fruit with paper towels so that the chocolate can set on it. Peel back the husks of the cape gooseberries to reveal the fruit but do not remove them.

3 Melt the chocolate in a bowl as directed on page 150. Remove from the heat just before fully melted and stir to complete the melting.

4 Dip each piece of fruit in the chocolate as directed on page 151 and put it on a baking sheet lined with waxed paper. Place the baking sheet in the refrigerator, to set the chocolate.

## VARIATIONS

**WHITE CHOCOLATE-COATED FRUIT:** Substitute *1/4 lb (125 g) white chocolate* for the bittersweet chocolate.

**CHOCOLATE & NUT-COATED FRUIT:** Spread *1/4 lb (125 g) chopped almonds* or *hazelnuts* on a flat surface. After dipping each piece of fruit in the melted chocolate, lightly roll the chocolate-coated part over the chopped nuts. Place the fruit on a baking sheet lined with waxed paper and place the sheet in the refrigerator, to set the chocolate.

**LIQUEUR-CHOCOLATE-COATED FRUIT:** Stir *1–2 tbsp liqueur of your choice, such as Grand Marnier or Cointreau,* into the melted chocolate before coating the fruit.

*Chocolate-coated Strawberries*

# DARK CHOCOLATE BOUCHEES

*Chocolate cups or cases with creamy fillings look fantastic
and are relatively easy to prepare. Vary the shapes and
fillings as much as possible so your bouchées look
professionally made.*
*Makes 24*

### INGREDIENTS

*1/4 lb (125 g) bittersweet chocolate,
broken into small pieces*
*1 egg yolk*
*1 tbsp butter, softened*
*1/2 cup (125 ml) whipping cream*
*24 chocolate cups made with 1/4 lb (125 g)
bittersweet chocolate (see page 150)*
*white chocolate curls (see page 151) for decoration*

### PREPARATION

**1** Melt the chocolate as directed on page 150.
When the chocolate has almost melted, add the
egg yolk and stir until the mixture is thick.
Remove from the heat.

**2** Take the bowl from the pan and let the chocolate
mixture cool slightly. Stir in the softened butter
and let the mixture cool until it reaches room
temperature. It should still be creamy.

**3** Meanwhile, whip the cream with a beater or an
electric mixer until stiff peaks form. Cut and
fold the cream into the cooled chocolate mixture.

**4** Fill the chocolate cups with the chocolate cream
(see page 150), and decorate with white
chocolate curls.

### VARIATIONS

**CREAMY CHOCOLATE & ORANGE BOUCHEES:**
Substitute *a combination of 2 oz (60 g) white chocolate
and 2 oz (60 g) bittersweet chocolate* for the 1/4 lb
(125 g) bittersweet chocolate. Add *1 tbsp finely
grated orange zest* to the melted chocolate with the
softened butter.

**WHITE CHOCOLATE & ORANGE BOUCHEES:**
Substitute *white chocolate* for the bittersweet
chocolate, and *triangular chocolate cases* for
the chocolate cups. Decorate with *orange zest
strips* instead of chocolate curls.

**COFFEE & NUT BOUCHEES:** Substitute *2 tbsp instant
coffee, dissolved in 2 tbsp boiling water,* for the
bittersweet chocolate. Decorate with *macadamia
nuts dipped in melted bittersweet chocolate* and *a sprig
of mint* instead of chocolate curls.

**MOCHA BOUCHEES:** Fill *diamond-shaped chocolate
cases* with the filling used in the Coffee & Nut
Bouchées (see above). Decorate with a sprinkling
of *coffee extract* instead of chocolate curls.

# CHOCOLATE TRUFFLES

*These irresistible chocolate balls can be made at least
2–3 days before serving.*
*Makes about 30*

### INGREDIENTS

*1 lb (500 g) bittersweet chocolate,
broken into small pieces*
*1/2 cup (125 g) superfine sugar*
*2 eggs*
*1 cup (200 g) butter, softened*
*3 tbsp cocoa powder*

### PREPARATION

**1** Melt the chocolate as directed on page 150.
Remove from the heat and add the eggs and
sugar, stirring vigorously until smooth. Return
to the heat and continue cooking over gentle heat
for 5 minutes, stirring constantly.

**2** Remove the bowl from the pan and beat in the
butter, 1 tbsp at a time, until the mixture is
smooth and thick. Refrigerate for 2–3 hours,
until firm.

**3** Scoop out about 1 tsp of the chilled chocolate
mixture on a cool work surface and, with your
hands dusted with cocoa powder, roll the
chocolate mixture into 1 1/2-in (3.5-cm) balls.

**4** Roll each truffle in cocoa powder to coat it
completely, then place in a paper case. Keep
chilled until ready to serve.

### VARIATIONS

**NUT TRUFFLES:** Toast *2 oz (60 g) shelled and husked
whole hazelnuts* in a 350°F (180°C) oven for about
5 minutes, until they are golden. Follow the recipe
for the Chocolate Truffles until the end of step 2.
Cover each hazelnut with the chocolate mixture,
roll into balls as directed in step 3 above, and
continue until the end of the recipe.

**RUM TRUFFLES:** Follow the recipe for the
Chocolate Truffles until the end of step 2, but do
not refrigerate. Add *1/4 cup (60 ml) dark rum* to the
mixture and continue until the end of the recipe.

**ORANGE LIQUEUR TRUFFLES:** Follow the recipe for
the Chocolate Truffles until the end of step 2, but
do not refrigerate. Add *3 tbsp orange liqueur, such as
Grand Marnier,* to the mixture and continue until
the end of the recipe.

# PETITS FOURS

Petits fours are small sweet cookies – traditionally baked at the end of the day in the *petit four*, the French for a small oven or at low heat. A selection of petits fours makes a decorative feature on a party table and are especially good to serve with fresh fruit, coffee, or liqueurs.

★

## ALMOND BISCOTTI

*Bite-sized biscotti make great finger food, much more convenient than the large, thick biscotti. The almond taste of these biscotti goes particularly well with sweet dessert wine or with espresso coffee.*
*Makes about 120*

### INGREDIENTS

*3/4 cup (125 g) almonds*
*2 eggs*
*1/4 cup (60 g) superfine sugar*
*1/4 cup (60 g) light brown sugar*
*1 tsp baking soda*
*1/4 tsp salt*
*21/4 cups (275 g) whole wheat or all-purpose flour,*
*or a combination*
*1 egg white*

### PREPARATION

1 Place the almonds on a baking sheet. Bake in a 375°F (190°C) oven for about 10 minutes, until golden brown and toasted. Remove from the oven and chop medium-fine with a knife (do not use a food processor, because it will either grind the almonds or leave large chunks). Leave the oven on.
2 Butter and flour a baking sheet. In a mixer, or food processor fitted with the metal blade, blend together the eggs and the sugars. Add the baking soda and salt, then gradually work in the flour.

3 Scrape the dough out onto a lightly floured work surface. Press out the dough and scatter the almonds over the top. Fold the dough over the nuts and knead gently until they are evenly distributed through the dough. Add a little more flour if the dough is sticky.
4 Divide the dough into quarters and shape each quarter into a long log, about 3/4 in (2 cm) wide and 1/2 in (1 cm) high.
5 Place the logs not too close together on the prepared baking sheet. Beat the egg white until it is foamy and brush it over the logs.
6 Bake the logs in the oven for 20 minutes, until golden brown.
7 Remove the logs from the oven and, with a long, serrated knife, cut them into diagonal slices about 1/4 in (5 mm) thick. Reduce the oven temperature to 275°F (140°C), and bake the slices for 30–40 minutes, until dry, hard, and lightly browned. Let cool.

### VARIATIONS

**GINGER BISCOTTI:** Add *2 tsp ground ginger* to the eggs and sugar before blending them together.
**BISCOTTI WITH RAISINS:** Substitute *raisins* for half the almonds. Add to the dough with the almonds.
**HONEY BISCOTTI:** Substitute *1/2 cup (125 ml) mild-flavored honey, such as clover or acacia,* for the sugars, and add up to *3/4 cup (90 g) extra flour.*

# Chocolate Chip Cookies

*Makes about 80*

### INGREDIENTS

1¼ cups (150 g) all-purpose flour
½ tsp baking soda
½ tsp salt
6 tbsp (90 g) unsalted butter, softened
¼ cup (60 g) superfine sugar
¼ cup (60 g) soft light brown sugar
1 egg, beaten
½ tsp vanilla extract (see page 156)
1 cup (150 g) chocolate chips

### PREPARATION

1 Sift together the flour, baking soda, and salt. Beat together the butter and sugars. Beat in the egg and vanilla extract. Gradually beat in the flour mixture. Stir in the chocolate chips.
2 Divide the dough in half and wrap each piece in waxed paper. Chill in the refrigerator for 1 hour, or place in the freezer for 20 minutes, until firm.
3 Flour your hands and shape the dough into logs 1 in (2.5 cm) in diameter. Wrap in lightly floured waxed paper and chill in the refrigerator for 1 hour.
4 Remove the logs from the refrigerator 1 at a time and cut into ¼-in (5-mm) thick slices. Place on ungreased baking sheets and bake in a 375° F (190°C) oven for about 8 minutes, until golden brown. Let stand for a few minutes. Transfer to wire racks and let cool.

 *Make batches of dough well in advance and freeze or chill them until ready to use.*

# Lemon Sables

*Sablé dough is great for making into different shapes for special occasions. For Christmas, it can be cut into stars, angels, or Christmas trees, while on Valentine's Day you can make hearts.*
*Makes about 36*

### INGREDIENTS

¾ cup (175 g) unsalted butter
¾ cup (175 g) superfine sugar
1 egg, beaten
2 tbsp finely chopped lemon zest
2 tbsp lemon juice
2½ cups (300 g) all-purpose flour
1 tsp baking powder
½ tsp salt

### PREPARATION

1 Mix the butter and sugar together in an electric mixer, or in a food processor fitted with the metal blade. Beat in the egg, lemon zest, and lemon juice.
2 Sift together the flour, baking powder, and salt. Add to the butter mixture and mix together. Gather the dough together into a ball and place in the refrigerator overnight or in the freezer for 1–2 hours.
3 Butter 2–3 baking sheets. Cut the dough into quarters and roll out each quarter on a lightly floured surface. Cut into small shapes and place on the prepared baking sheets.
4 Bake in a 350°F (180°C) oven for 10 minutes, until lightly browned. Transfer to wire racks and let cool.

# Coconut Tuiles

*Makes about 25*

### INGREDIENTS

5 tbsp (75 g) softened butter, more for greasing
1 cup (125 g) confectioners' sugar (or icing sugar), sifted
3 egg whites
9 tbsp (75 g) all-purpose flour, sifted
2 tsp heavy cream
2 tbsp shredded coconut

### PREPARATION

1 Cream the butter with the confectioners' sugar (or icing sugar) until pale and creamy. Add about half the egg whites and beat well.
2 Gradually stir in the flour, remaining egg whites, and the cream. Beat until the mixture is smooth.
3 Grease a baking sheet with butter and put small spoonfuls of the tuile mixture at large intervals on the sheet. Sprinkle the shredded coconut over the edges of the tuiles.
4 Bake in a 400°F (200°C) oven for about 5 minutes, or until the tuiles are a delicate golden color.
5 Remove from the oven and immediately slide a spatula under the tuiles to prevent them from sticking. Place the tuiles on a greased rolling pin, coconut side up, and let stand on their edges until set.

# A SUMMER PARTY

*Fresh flavors and crisp textures complement the heat of summer.*
*Barbecued kebabs are ideal for an outdoor party and*
*fresh fruit and vegetables are a must.*

**Vegetable crudités**
**and Creamy**
**Curried Dip (page 29)**

**Choux Puffs (page 138),**
**with Goat Cheese**
**& Pepper filling**
**(page 50)**

*Tuna & Red Pepper Kebabs (page 99)*
*Shrimp & Pepper Kebabs (page 98)*

*Cherry Tomato Cups*
*(page 148) stuffed with Basil*
*Pesto (page 25)*

*Fresh Fruit Tartlets*
*(page 114)*

# SPONGE CAKES & MERINGUES

*These dainty confections are welcome at any party. Sponge cakes are quick and economical to make. Cut them into a variety of shapes with a pastry cutter, and layer or top them with creamy fillings. Meringues and macaroons are ideal when serving large numbers because they can be made weeks in advance. Decorate them with brightly colored fruit, icings, and fillings for an eye-catching presentation.*

★

## CHOCOLATE FANCIES

*In this recipe, Sponge Cake is layered and then cut into small squares to make delicious little cakes.*
*Makes 16*

### INGREDIENTS

*8-in (20-cm) square Sponge Cake (see page 152)*
*7 oz (200 g) white chocolate, broken into small pieces*
**FOR THE VANILLA BUTTERCREAM FILLING**
*2 cups (250 g) confectioners' sugar (or icing sugar), sifted*
*3 tbsp butter, softened*
*1 1/2 tbsp milk*
*1 tsp vanilla extract (see page 156)*

### PREPARATION

1 Cut the cake horizontally into 2 layers.
2 Make the vanilla buttercream filling: Mix the ingredients together with an electric mixer, until smooth and fluffy.
3 Using a spatula, spread the buttercream over 1 layer of the cake. Place the second sponge layer on top and chill in the refrigerator for 5 minutes.
4 Melt the chocolate as directed on page 150.
5 Cut the cake into 16 x 2-in (5-cm) squares with a knife that has been dipped in hot water and dried. Make sure that the edges are neat.
6 Set a wire rack over a baking sheet. Space the cakes on the rack and pour the melted chocolate over to cover them evenly. Let the excess chocolate drip onto the baking sheet (it can be scraped off and reused if required). Let the chocolate set.
7 Put the remaining buttercream into a paper pastry bag (see page 151), and pipe a decoration on top of each cake.

### VARIATION

**MINI FRUIT SANDWICHES:** Spread a layer of *fruit jam* over the cake before the buttercream filling. Cut the chilled layered cake into 16 rounds with a 2-in (5-cm) pastry cutter. Decorate with *fresh fruit* and *whipped cream.*

## CHOCOLATE MERINGUES

*Makes 18*

### INGREDIENTS

*4 egg whites*
*1 cup (250 g) superfine sugar*
*1/4 lb (125 g) semisweet chocolate, broken into small pieces, for the topping*
**FOR THE GANACHE FILLING**
*1/4 lb (125 g) semisweet chocolate, broken into small pieces*
*1/2 cup (125 ml) heavy cream*

### PREPARATION

1 Beat the egg whites using an electric beater, until soft peaks form. Add the superfine sugar, 1 tbsp at a time, and continue beating until it is fully incorporated and the mixture is stiff and shiny.
2 Put the meringue mixture into a pastry bag fitted with a small star tube. Pipe the mixture into 36 x 2-in (5-cm) small rosettes on baking sheets lined with waxed paper.
3 Bake the meringues in a 250°F (120°C) oven for 1 hour, or until the meringues are firm and can be lifted easily off the paper. Turn off the oven and leave the meringues in the oven until cold.
4 Make the ganache filling: Put the chocolate pieces into a bowl. Bring the cream just to a boil, pour over the chocolate pieces, and stir until the chocolate has melted. Beat the mixture with an electric beater for about 5 minutes, until the ganache mixture is fluffy and has cooled.
5 Melt the chocolate for the topping as directed on page 150.
6 Drizzle the melted chocolate from a fork over the tops of the meringues, then let the chocolate set for 5–10 minutes.
7 Sandwich the meringues together in pairs with the ganache filling.

# FRUIT MERINGUES

*The combination of whisked egg whites, whipped cream, and fresh fruit is irresistible — as in these "mini Pavlovas," which are illustrated below.*
*Makes 35*

### INGREDIENTS

*4 egg whites*
*1 cup (250 g) superfine sugar*
*1 cup (250 ml) heavy cream*
*2 tbsp lemon curd (optional)*
*fresh fruit, such as strawberries, blueberries, raspberries, oranges, and kiwi fruit*
*sprigs of mint for decoration (optional)*

### PREPARATION

1 Beat the egg whites using an electric beater, until soft peaks form. Add the sugar, 1 tbsp at a time, and continue beating until it is fully incorporated and the mixture is stiff and shiny.
2 Put the meringue mixture into a pastry bag fitted with a small 1/2-in (1-cm) tube. Pipe the mixture into 35 x 2-in (5-cm) rounds on baking sheets lined with waxed paper.
3 Bake the meringues in a 250°F (120°C) oven for 1 hour, or until the meringues are firm and can be lifted easily off the paper. Turn off the oven and leave the meringues in the oven until cold.
4 Whip the cream until it forms stiff peaks, then fold in the lemon curd if using. Spoon a little cream onto each meringue round, top with fresh fruit, and decorate with mint sprigs if using.

# COFFEE MACAROONS

*Macaroons, originally from Venice, have been made for centuries. In this recipe, they are sandwiched together with buttercream filling.*
*Makes about 45*

### INGREDIENTS

*2 cups (250 g) confectioners' sugar (or icing sugar)*
*2 cups (200 g) ground almonds*
*3 egg whites*
*1 tbsp superfine sugar*
*2 tsp instant coffee dissolved in*
*1 tbsp boiling water*
**FOR THE COFFEE BUTTERCREAM FILLING**
*1 cup (125 g) confectioners' sugar (or icing sugar), sifted*
*1/2 cup (125 g) butter*
*2 tsp instant coffee dissolved in*
*1 tbsp boiling water*

### PREPARATION

1 Sift the confectioners' sugar (or icing sugar) and ground almonds together. Beat the egg whites and superfine sugar with a metal whisk or an electric mixer until stiff. Stir in the coffee.
2 Gently cut and fold the sugar and almond mixture into the eggwhite mixture with a metal spoon.
3 Put the macaroon mixture into a pastry bag fitted with a 1/2-in (1-cm) tube. Pipe the mixture into about 90 x 1-in (2.5-cm) rounds on baking sheets lined with waxed paper.
4 Bake in a 400°F (200°C) oven for about 12 minutes or until a light crust forms. Let cool slightly, then peel the macaroons off the paper. Transfer to a wire rack and let cool completely.
5 Make the buttercream filling: Beat the confectioners' sugar (or icing sugar) and the butter together with an electric mixer for 10 minutes, or until fluffy. Gradually beat in the coffee.
6 Sandwich the macaroons together in pairs with the coffee buttercream filling.

**Orange & Kiwi Fruit Meringues**

**Strawberry Meringues**

**Blueberry Meringues**

# FRESH FRUIT PLATTERS

Colorful and refreshing fruit platters should have a prominent place on a party table. The fruit can be served *au nature*, or with a selection of creamy dips as illustrated here. Choose fruits that are easy to handle – they shouldn't drip – and have plenty of toothpicks on hand for spearing them.

## SUMMER FRUIT PLATTER

*Serves 12*

### INGREDIENTS

1 ripe honeydew melon
1-lb (500-g) piece of watermelon
1 ripe pineapple
2¹/2 cups (500 g) ripe strawberries, with hulls
8–10 apricots
4 medium ripe but firm peaches
3–4 ripe but firm nectarines
6–8 fresh figs
1 lb (500 g) cherries, with stems
Creamy Dips of your choice (see page 134)

### PREPARATION

**1** Using a melon baller, scoop out balls from the flesh of both the melons.
**2** Peel the pineapple and quarter it lengthwise. Cut off the core from each piece and then cut the pineapple into bite-sized pieces.
**3** Halve the strawberries lengthwise. Halve and pit the apricots. Halve, pit, and slice the peaches and nectarines. Quarter the figs lengthwise.
**4** Distribute the fruit over platters and serve the dips in individual bowls.

### VARIATIONS

**MEXICAN FRUIT PLATTER** (see page 101): Combine *1 lb (500 g) watermelon chunks* with *4 mangoes, peeled, pitted, and sliced; 6 passion fruit, halved;* and *2 star fruit, sliced crosswise.* Spear *1 lb (500 g) pineapple chunks* on toothpicks, dip in *melted chocolate,* and use to fill *6 large papaya halves.*

**ASIAN FRUIT PLATTER** (see pages 86–87): Combine *1 lb fresh litchis, peeled,* with *2 papayas, peeled, seeded, and cut into ¹/2-in (1-cm) dice; 12 mandarin oranges, peeled and segmented; 2 prickly pears, quartered lengthwise; 2 large Asian pears, cut into chevrons; 2 star fruit, sliced crosswise; 6 passion fruit, halved; 2 pomegranates, quartered lengthwise;* and *12 kumquats, halved lengthwise.*

*Orange & Cointreau Dip*

*Pistachio Dip*

*Chocolate Dip*

*Ginger Dip*

# CREAMY DIPS

*Whipped cream sweetened with a little sugar is the simplest dip to serve with fresh fruit. Crème Anglaise can also be served as a dip. It takes a little more time and trouble than simply whipping cream, but it does add a touch of luxury to a platter of fresh fruit. Serve it plain (see page 153) or flavor it as in the recipes here. All these dips will keep for 1 day in the refrigerator.*

★

## ORANGE & COINTREAU DIP

*Makes about 1 1/4 cups (300 ml)*

### INGREDIENTS

*2 tbsp whipping cream*
*2 tbsp Cointreau or other orange-flavored liqueur*
*finely grated zest of 1 orange*
*1 cup (250 ml) Crème Anglaise (see page 153), cooled*

### PREPARATION

1 Whip the cream just until it holds its shape.
2 Stir the Cointreau and grated orange zest into the Crème Anglaise, then fold in the whipped cream until evenly incorporated.

## GINGER DIP

*Makes about 1 1/4 cups (300 ml)*

### INGREDIENTS

*1/4–1/2 tsp ground ginger*
*1/4 tsp vanilla extract (see page 156)*
*1 cup (250 ml) Crème Anglaise (see page 153), cooled*
*2 tbsp whipping cream*

### PREPARATION

1 Stir the ground ginger and vanilla extract into the Crème Anglaise until evenly mixed.
2 Whip the cream just until it holds its shape. Fold into the Crème Anglaise mixture until evenly incorporated.

## CHOCOLATE DIP

*Makes about 1 1/4 cups (300 ml)*

### INGREDIENTS

*3 oz (90 g) semisweet chocolate, broken into small pieces*
*1 cup (250 ml) Crème Anglaise (see page 153)*
*2 tbsp whipping cream*

### PREPARATION

1 Put the chocolate pieces in a bowl placed over a saucepan of gently simmering water and heat gently until melted. Remove the bowl from the pan and let the chocolate cool, for about 5 minutes.
2 Stir the melted chocolate into the Crème Anglaise until evenly blended. Let cool.
3 Whip the cream just until it holds its shape. Fold into the Crème Anglaise mixture until evenly incorporated.

## PISTACHIO DIP

*Makes about 1 1/4 cups (300 ml)*

### INGREDIENTS

*2 oz (60 g) shelled and skinned pistachios*
*1 cup (250 ml) Crème Anglaise (see page 153), cooled*
*2 tbsp whipping cream*
*green food coloring (optional)*

### PREPARATION

1 Process the pistachios in a food processor fitted with the metal blade until very finely ground. Press through a strainer with a metal spoon into the Crème Anglaise. Beat well to mix.
2 Whip the cream just until it holds its shape.
3 Fold the whipped cream into the Crème Anglaise mixture until evenly incorporated, adding 1–2 drops food coloring, if you wish.

# TECHNIQUES

*Here are the basic techniques and recipes on which
many of the finger foods and appetizers in this book
are based. You will find inspirational ideas for simple
vegetable containers and beautiful garnishes.
Instructions are given to help you prepare pastries
for quiches, tartlets, choux puffs, and gougères, and
doughs for pizza and focaccia. Recipes and
instructions are included for blini, crêpes, and phyllo
shapes as well as for sponge cakes. Clever ways with
chocolate are also explained. Step-by-step
illustrations make each recipe easy to follow.*

# PASTRIES

The main ingredient of pastry is flour. Fat, eggs, and water are added in varying proportions for flavor, color, and texture. Use Pâte Brisée or Yeasted Olive Oil Pastry for quiches, and Pâte Sucrée or rich and crumbly Rough Puff Pastry for sweet tartlets. Fill choux puffs with cream, or add cheese to the dough for gougères.

★

## PATE BRISEE

*You can make Pâte Brisée from all-purpose flour or whole wheat flour. Whole wheat pastry will have a much nuttier flavor than Pâte Brisée, but it is a little trickier to roll out because it tends to crumble.*
*Enough for 8–10 x 3-in (7-cm) quiche shells*

### INGREDIENTS

*1½ cups (175 g) all-purpose flour,*
*or 1½ cups (175 g) whole wheat flour,*
*or ⅔ cup (90 g) whole wheat flour*
*and ⅔ cup (90 g) all-purpose flour*
*¼ tsp salt*
*6 tbsp (90 g) cold butter, cut into small pieces*
*2–3 tbsp iced water*

*1 Combine the flour and salt in a large bowl. Quickly cut in the butter and roll briskly between the palms of your hands to make sure that the butter is evenly distributed. The mixture should have the consistency of crumbs.*

*2 Add 1 tbsp water at a time to the dry mixture and blend with a fork until the dough comes together. Shape the dough into a ball. Refrigerate for 20 minutes or longer.*

*3 When ready to use the dough, place the ball on a lightly floured work surface, and press it down gently with your fingertips so that it is about 1 in (2.5 cm) thick.*

## ROLLING OUT DOUGH & LINING QUICHE PANS

To roll out dough, lightly dust the rolling pin and work surface with flour to prevent sticking. A cool surface, such as marble, is especially good. Roll out the dough in one direction only, without stretching it, otherwise it will shrink during baking. Handle the dough as little as possible: if it becomes elastic, it will be difficult to roll out.

Roll out whole wheat dough between waxed paper to prevent cracking.

*1 Roll out the dough into a 12-in (30-cm) round. Cut rounds with appropriate pastry cutters, depending on the size of the finished tartlets.*

*2 Line pans with dough rounds, and gently press into the edges of the pans. Refrigerate, covered, for 2 hours to relax the pastry.*

# YEASTED OLIVE OIL PASTRY

*This dough is very light compared to a butter dough, and is extremely easy to work with.*
*Enough for 8–10 x 3-in (7-cm) quiche shells*

## INGREDIENTS

*¼ cup (60 ml) lukewarm water*
*1 tsp dried yeast*
*1¼ cups (150 g) whole wheat flour*
*1¼ cups (150 g) all-purpose flour*
*½–¾ tsp salt*
*1 large egg*
*¼ cup (60 ml) olive oil*

## Making Pastry Dough in a Machine

**For Pâte Brisée,** *place the flour or flours and salt in a food processor fitted with the metal blade. Pulse a few times to combine the ingredients. Add the butter in small pieces and pulse on and off about 30 times, until the mixture resembles crumbs. With the machine running, add the water, 1 tbsp at a time. As soon as the dough comes together, remove from the food processor and shape into a ball.*

**For Yeasted Olive Oil Pastry,** *follow step 1 of the recipe, then, using the paddle, combine all the ingredients in the bowl of an electric mixer. Switch to the dough hook and continue mixing until the dough comes together; remove, and shape into a ball.*

*1* Put the lukewarm water in a small bowl, sprinkle over the yeast, and let stand for 5–10 minutes, until the yeast dissolves to a smooth paste.

*2* In a large bowl, combine the flours with salt to taste, and stir in the yeast mixture. Beat in the egg and olive oil. Work into a dough, and knead for a few minutes, then shape into a ball.

*3* Place in a lightly oiled bowl, cover, and set in a warm place to rise for 2 hours. The dough will not rise much, but it will expand and soften. Remove and punch it down gently. Cover, and let rest for 10 minutes.

## PRESSING DOUGH INTO QUICHE PANS

Instead of being rolled out, pastry dough can be pressed directly into pans. This method is particularly useful for whole wheat pastry dough, which can break when being rolled out. Divide the dough into the same number of portions as quiche pans, form into balls, and pat out into rounds to fit the pans. For a large quiche, press the dough out toward the side with the heel of your hand. For smaller quiches, use your fingertips.

*1* Divide the dough into pieces. Shape into balls and press them flat between the palms of your hands. Place a round of dough in each pan.

*2* Using your fingertips, spread the dough out from the center of the pan toward the side. Cover loosely and let rest for 20–30 minutes.

# CHOUX PASTRY

*Enough for 40 x 1 1/2-in (3.5-cm) choux puffs or gougères*

## INGREDIENTS

1 cup (250 ml) water
6 tbsp (90 g) unsalted butter
1 tsp superfine sugar
salt
1 1/4 cups (150 g) all-purpose flour, sifted
4 large eggs

**FOR GOUGERES**
1/2 cup (60 g) grated Gruyère cheese

*1* Put the water, butter, sugar, and a pinch of salt into a 6-cup (1.5-liter) pan and bring to a boil. Reduce the heat slightly and simmer gently until the butter has melted.

*2* Remove from the heat and add the flour all at once, stirring vigorously and constantly with a wooden spoon. Return to a medium-high heat and stir until the mixture comes away from the side of the pan in a mass and a film forms on the bottom of the pan.

*3* Remove from the heat. Add 1 egg and beat in well. Beat the remaining eggs into the paste 1 at a time, then beat until the mixture is soft and shiny. (For gougères, reserve 2 tbsp cheese for topping, and beat in 1/4 of the remainder with each egg.)

## PIPING & BAKING CHOUX PASTRY

*1* Fill a pastry bag fitted with a 1 1/2-in (3.5-cm) star tube with choux paste. On buttered baking sheets, pipe 3-in (7-cm) lengths for gougères, or 1 1/2-in (3.5-cm) mounds for puffs, spaced apart.

*2* Brush the tops carefully with beaten egg. Bake in the upper and lower thirds of a 425°F (220°C) oven for 20 minutes, until golden brown and doubled in size.

*3* Remove the pastries and pierce along one side with a sharp knife. Turn off the oven and return the pastries to the oven for another 10 minutes with the door ajar. Remove and cool on racks.

# ROUGH PUFF PASTRY

*The method given here is easier and quicker than the classic puff pastry method, but it still has plenty of buttery, feathery layers. Use the pastry to make tart or tartlet shells (see box, below) and fill with fresh fruit, or use for Napoleons, palmiers, or other ornamental pastries.*
*Enough for 2 x 10-in (25-cm) tarts or 36 small tartlets*

## INGREDIENTS

1¼ cups (300 g) unsalted butter, chopped and chilled
2½ cups (300 g) all-purpose flour, sifted with ½ tsp salt
5–6 tbsp iced water

*1 Divide the butter into 4 equal portions. Rub 1 portion into the flour until evenly distributed. Add the water, 1 tbsp at a time, and blend with a fork until the dough can be gathered up into a ball. Wrap and refrigerate for 30 minutes.*

*2 Roll out the dough into a rectangle ½-in (1-cm) thick. Scatter ⅓ of the remaining butter over ⅔ of the dough. Fold over the unbuttered ⅓, then fold over again to cover the remaining exposed buttered portion.*

*3 Turn the package over and seal the 2 narrow ends together with a rolling pin. Wrap and refrigerate for 15–30 minutes.*

*4 Remove from the refrigerator, unwrap, and roll out into a rectangle ½-in (1-cm) thick. Repeat step 2, using ½ of the remaining butter, and then step 3.*

*5 Remove from the refrigerator, unwrap, and roll out as in step 4. Repeat step 2, using the remaining butter, and then step 3.*

*6 Remove from the refrigerator, unwrap, and repeat step 2 without butter. Wrap and refrigerate for at least 15–30 minutes, or preferably for longer (2 hours or until ready to use).*

## MAKING PASTRY SHELLS

*Remove the dough from the refrigerator and divide into 2 equal pieces for large tarts or 4 pieces for tartlets. Roll out to ⅛– ¼-in (2.5–5-mm) thickness. For tartlets, cut out 36 rounds. Line tart or tartlet pans (prick the pastry for large tarts) and refrigerate for 15–30 minutes. Brush with egg glaze, and bake in a 400°F (200°C) oven for 10 minutes, then at 350°F (180°C) for another 10–20 minutes.*

## PATE SUCREE

*This is a sweet pastry for dessert tarts or tartlets. Enough for 1 x 10- x 12-in (25- x 30-cm) or 1 x 10-in (25-cm) tart shell, or 24 x 2-in (5-cm) or 16 x 3-in (7-cm) tartlet shells*

### INGREDIENTS

*1¹/₂ cups (175 g) all-purpose flour, sifted*
*1–2 tbsp superfine sugar (use the larger amount*
*if you prefer a sweeter pastry)*
*¹/₄ tsp salt*
*6 tbsp (90 g) unsalted butter*
*2–3 tbsp iced water*

### PREPARATION

**1** Place the flour, sugar, and salt in a large bowl and combine well.
**2** Quickly cut the butter into the mixture and roll the mixture briskly between the palms of your hands to make sure the butter is evenly distributed. The mixture should have the consistency of crumbs.
**3** Add the water, 1 tbsp at a time, and blend with a fork until the dough forms a ball.
**4** Place the dough on a sheet of lightly floured waxed paper. Press it down so that it is about 1 in (2.5 cm) thick and cover with another sheet of lightly floured waxed paper. Refrigerate for 20 minutes or longer before rolling out.

---

### MAKING PASTRY DOUGH IN A FOOD PROCESSOR

*Place the dry ingredients in the bowl of a food processor fitted with the metal blade. Pulse a few times. Cut the butter into small pieces and add to the bowl. Pulse on and off about 30 times, until the mixture resembles crumbs. With the machine running, add the almond extract, if using in the Almond Dessert Pastry, and the water, 1 tbsp at a time. As soon as the dough comes together, stop the machine and remove the dough. Shape into a ball.*

---

## ALMOND DESSERT PASTRY

*This dessert pastry has a rich, nutty flavor. I use it more often than Pâte Sucrée, especially for fruit tarts. It is slightly more difficult to roll out, so place a piece of waxed paper over the dough when you roll it. Enough for 1 x 10-in (25-cm) tart shell, 16 x 2-in (5-cm) or 10 x 3-in (7-cm) tartlet shells*

### INGREDIENTS

*¹/₂ cup (60 g) ground almonds*
*1 cup (125 g) all-purpose flour, sifted*
*2 tbsp superfine sugar*
*¹/₄ tsp salt*
*6 tbsp (90 g) unsalted butter*
*1 drop of almond extract (optional) see page 156*
*2–3 tbsp iced water*

### PREPARATION

**1** Place the ground almonds, flour, sugar, and salt in a large bowl and combine well.
**2** Quickly cut the butter into the mixture and roll the mixture briskly between the palms of your hands to make sure the butter is evenly distributed. The mixture should have the consistency of crumbs.
**3** Add the almond extract if using, and the water, 1 tbsp at a time, and blend in with a fork until you can gather the dough into a ball.
**4** Place the dough on a sheet of lightly floured waxed paper. Press it down so that it is about 1 in (2.5 cm) thick and cover with another sheet of lightly floured waxed paper. Refrigerate for 1 hour or longer before rolling out.

*Both Pâte Sucrée and Almond Dessert Pastry can be chilled in the refrigerator for up to 4 days. They can also be frozen, before rolling out or after making tart or tartlet shells, for 3 months. Transfer frozen pastry shells directly from the freezer to the oven for prebaking.*

## LINING TARTLET PANS WITH SWEET PASTRY

Pâte Sucrée and Almond Dessert Pastry are quite crumbly because of the sugar and ground nut content, so they can be difficult to roll out. Your work surface should be cold – marble is ideal, but ceramic and granite are also good.

Remove the dough from the refrigerator. If the dough is too firm to roll easily, knock it with the rolling pin to make it more pliable. Dust the work surface and rolling pin lightly with flour. Place a sheet of waxed paper over the dough to prevent it from cracking, and roll out in one direction only, to ¼-in (5-mm) thickness. Do not stretch the dough, because this will cause shrinkage during baking.

*1 Cut out rounds using an appropriate pastry cutter, depending on the size of the finished tartlets. Use a firm downward action, without twisting, to prevent stretching the dough. Ease each round gently off the work surface with a spatula and place in a pan.*

*2 Gently press the rounds into the edges of the pans. Run a rolling pin over the edge of each pan and trim off the extra pastry. Prick the bottoms of the shells in several places. Refrigerate, covered, for 2 hours or double wrap and freeze for up to 3 months.*

## MAKING A LARGE RECTANGULAR TART SHELL

One large tart is much easier to make, fill, and bake than a number of small tartlets, and it can easily be cut into bite-sized pieces.

However, you may find a large piece of dough difficult to roll out. To make it more manageable, make sure the dough is well chilled and handle it as little as possible.

Dust the work surface and rolling pin lightly with flour. Place a sheet of waxed paper over the dough to prevent it from cracking, and roll out in one direction only, to ¼-in (5-mm) thickness. Do not stretch the dough, because this will cause shrinkage during baking.

*1 Lift the dough onto a rolling pin and unroll it onto a lightly greased 12-x 10-in (30-x 25-cm) baking pan.*

*2 Fit the dough into the corners and up the sides of the pan, smoothing out wrinkles with a small ball of dough.*

---

### BAKING TART & TARTLET SHELLS

*To bake tart and tartlet shells blind, line the shells loosely with foil, shiny side up. With your fingertips, push the foil into the edges and corners of the pastry to prevent it from shrinking during baking. Weight the foil down with baking beans or rice.*

*For partially baked pastry shells, bake 10-in (25-cm) tart shells in a 375°F (190°C) oven for 20 minutes, and 2–3-in (5–7-cm) tartlet shells for 10 minutes, until the edges of the pastry are lightly browned. Remove the foil and*

*beans and bake for a further 10 minutes for a tart shell, or 5 minutes for tartlet shells, until the crust is golden.*

*For fully baked pastry shells, bake tart shells for a further 20 minutes, or tartlet shells for a further 10 minutes, until they are browned. Remove from the oven and let cool on racks for 5–10 minutes, until you can handle the shells without breaking them, then carefully remove the pastry shells from the pans.*

# Phyllo Shapes

Paper-thin phyllo pastry can be wrapped around delicious savory fillings (see pages 76–77) in a variety of shapes: classic *tiropites* or triangles, money bags with scrunched tops, tubular cigars, or little square parcels tied up with a pretty garnish.

Brush with melted butter and olive oil at all stages and especially the finished pastry. Keep pastry you are not working with wrapped in a damp dish towel. Phyllo pastry is available ready-made, but if you have trouble finding it, you could make it yourself (see page 143).

★

## TIROPITES (TRIANGLES)

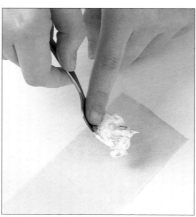

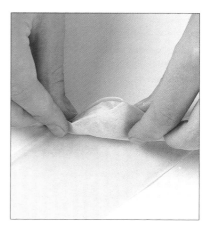

*1* With a sharp knife, cut 2¹/2-in (6-cm) wide strips from the length of each sheet of phyllo pastry. Brush each strip with a mixture of melted butter and olive oil.

*2* Place 1 tsp of the chosen filling at one end of a strip. Lifting a corner, fold the pastry diagonally over the filling until the shorter edge of the strip meets the longer edge.

*3* Continue folding over and over, alternately at right angles, then diagonally, until you reach the end of the strip. Seal and brush with more melted-butter-and-olive-oil mixture.

## MONEY BAGS

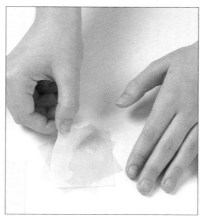

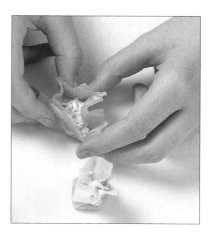

*1* With a sharp knife, cut 2¹/2-in (6-cm) wide strips from the length of each sheet of phyllo pastry. Cut each strip into 2¹/2-in (6-cm) squares.

*2* Brush a square of pastry with a mixture of melted butter and olive oil and place another square on it at an angle. Grease again and repeat with a third square to form a 12-pointed star.

*3* Place 1 tsp of the chosen filling in the center of the pastry and bring all the corners together around it. Twist to secure, and brush with more melted butter-and-olive-oil mixture.

## CIGARS

 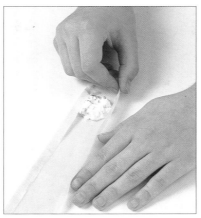 

*1* With a sharp knife, cut 2¹/2-in (6-cm) wide strips from each sheet of phyllo pastry. Brush the long edges with melted butter and olive oil.

*2* Place 1 tsp of the filling, centered, near one end of a strip. Fold the long edges over the filling and along the length of the strip.

*3* Fold the short end over the filling and continue rolling until you reach the end. Seal and brush the cigars with the melted butter and olive oil.

## PARCELS

*1* Brush a 2¹/2-in (6-cm) square of phyllo pastry with melted butter and olive oil. Place 1 tsp filling in the center and fold over one of the edges.

*2* Fold the opposite edge over the filling to overlap the first edge. Brush with melted butter and olive oil. Fold over a third edge and brush again.

*3* Fold the final edge over in the opposite direction, so that the filling is covered with equal layers of pastry on either side. Brush again.

---

### *MAKING PHYLLO PASTRY BY HAND*

*Enough for about 60 pastries*

#### INGREDIENTS

*2 cups (250 g) all-purpose flour, more for dusting*
*1 egg, beaten*
*2 tbsp canola or sunflower oil*
*¹/4 cup (60 ml) warm water*

#### PREPARATION

**1** Sift together the flour and a pinch of salt. Add the egg, oil, and water. Mix to a soft, sticky dough.

**2** Turn the dough onto a floured surface and knead for 5–7 minutes, until smooth and shiny. Cover with a bowl and let stand for 30 minutes.

**3** Lightly flour the work surface and the dough, and roll out the dough into a large square. Cover with a damp dish towel and let stand for 15 minutes. Place floured hands under the dough and stretch it out from the center until it is about 1 yard (1 meter) square.

# BASIC PIZZA & FOCACCIA

Pizza and focaccia doughs are both made with yeast. They require kneading, to build up the gluten content that binds the dough, and they need to rest in a warm place, so that the yeast can work on the dough to make it rise.

★

## MAKING A PIZZA BASE

*This dough is very easy to handle. Use it to make large or medium pizzas, small pizzettas, or calzone (see pages 63–67). The rolled-out dough can be baked either in pizza pans or directly on a baking stone (see page 156).*
*Makes 2 large pizzas, 3 medium pizzas, 16–20 pizzettas, or 36 calzone*

### INGREDIENTS

*2 tsp dried yeast*
*1 1/2 cups (350 ml) lukewarm water*
*4 1/3 cups (560 g) all-purpose flour, plus 1/2 cup (60 g), as necessary, for kneading*
*2 tsp salt*

*1 Dissolve the yeast in 1/4 cup (60 ml) of the water, and let stand for 5 minutes, until the yeast begins to bubble. Mix in the remaining water.*

*2 Mix 1 cup (125g) of the flour with the salt, and stir in. Fold in the remaining flour, about 1/2 cup (60 g) at a time, until the dough holds its shape.*

*3 Knead the dough on a floured surface for 10 minutes, adding flour as necessary, until the dough becomes very elastic. Shape into a ball.*

*4 Place the dough in a bowl lightly oiled with olive oil, and roll it around in the bowl to coat with the oil. Cover with a dish towel, and set in a warm place to rise for 1 1/2–2 hours, or until the dough doubles in volume.*

*5 Punch down the dough and divide it into the number of pieces required (see above). Roll out each piece no thicker than 1/4 in (5 mm). Keep the other pieces covered with a damp dish towel.*

*6 Oil baking sheets or pizza pans, and sprinkle with cornmeal or semolina. For pizzas and pizzettas, roll the edges of the dough in and pinch a lip all the way around.*

## MAKING FOCACCIA

*Focaccia dough is more moist than pizza dough, and, therefore, slightly more unwieldy. The finished breads should be about 1 in (2.5 cm) thick, and soft.*
*Makes 2 x 10¹/₂- x 15¹/₂-in (26- x 38-cm) rectangular focaccias*

### INGREDIENTS

*2 tsp dried yeast*
*2 cups (500 ml) lukewarm water*
*¹/₄ cup (60 ml) olive oil*
*5–6 cups (650–750 g) all-purpose flour, or 3 cups (375 g) all-purpose flour and 3 cups (375 g) whole wheat flour, plus additional all-purpose flour for kneading*
*2¹/₂ tsp salt*
*1 tbsp olive oil, for brushing the tops*

*1 Dissolve the yeast in the water, and let stand for 10 minutes. Stir in the olive oil.*

*2 Combine the flour and salt, and fold in all but 1 cup (150 g) of it, until the dough holds its shape.*

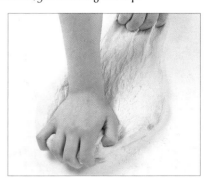

*3 Knead on a lightly floured surface for 10 minutes, adding flour, until the dough is elastic. Shape into a ball.*

*4 Roll in a bowl lightly oiled with olive oil. Cover with a damp dish towel, and let rise in a warm place for 1¹/₂–2 hours, or until doubled in size.*

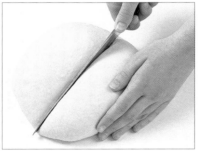

*5 Turn out onto a lightly floured work surface, knead for 1 minute, then cut into 2 pieces. Shape into 2 balls.*

*6 Oil 2 baking sheets and dust with cornmeal. Roll or press out the dough to just about fit the sheets. Cover, and let rest for 10 minutes*

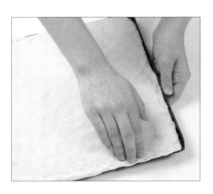

*7 Press the dough out to the edges of the baking sheets. Cover with damp dish towels, and let rise for 1 hour, until the dough is puffed up.*

*8 Dimple the tops all over, and brush lightly with olive oil. Bake in a 400°F (200°C) oven, preferably with a baking stone in it (see page 156), for 20–25 minutes, until the tops are golden brown. Cool on racks.*

### MAKING PIZZA & FOCACCIA IN AN ELECTRIC MIXER

*Dissolve the yeast in the mixer bowl; let stand for 10 minutes. Stir in the oil. If making focaccia, reserve 3 oz (90 g) of the flour. Mix the flour and salt into the yeast mixture with the mixing attachment. Knead for 2 minutes with the dough hook at low speed, then for 10 minutes at medium speed, adding more flour for focaccia. Knead for 1 minute by hand and shape into a ball. Continue from step 4.*

# BLINI & CREPES

These are both made from egg-and-milk batters. Blini batter has yeast added to it, which makes the blini thick and spongy.

Crêpe batter is thinner, and it is spread around the pan so that the finished crêpe is thin enough to wrap around a filling.

★

## BLINI

*You can make blini from buckwheat or fine cornmeal. Buckwheat blini will be darker than cornmeal — they are excellent for fish toppings. Cornmeal blini are grainier, and well suited to Mexican style toppings. A heavy griddle is best for cooking blini, but you can also cook them in a crêpe pan or a nonstick skillet. Makes 50 x 2-in (5-cm) blini*

### INGREDIENTS

*1 tsp dried yeast*
*2 tbsp lukewarm water*
*1 cup plus 2 tbsp (275 ml) lukewarm milk*
*1 cup (125 g) stoneground cornmeal or buckwheat flour*
*1 cup (125 g) all-purpose flour*
*3/4—1 tsp salt*
*1/2 cup (125 ml) buttermilk or plain nonfat yogurt*
*2 large eggs, separated*
*2 tbsp unsalted butter, melted*

*1 Dissolve the yeast in the water in a bowl. Stir in the milk and let stand for 5 minutes. Combine the cornmeal or buckwheat flour and the all-purpose flour with salt to taste, and gradually add to the milk. Mix well. Stir in the buttermilk or yogurt.*

*2 Beat the egg yolks into the batter. Cover, and set in a warm place to rise for 1 hour or until the batter is quite bubbly and spongy.*

*3 Beat the egg whites to soft peaks and gently fold into the batter. Cover again, and let rise for 1 hour. The batter should be spongy and light.*

*4 Lightly grease a pan with the melted butter and heat over medium heat. Pour in 1—2 tbsp batter for each blini.*

*5 Cook for about 1 minute, until bubbles break through. Using a metal spatula, turn the blini, and brown on the other side for 30 seconds.*

*6 Overlap the blini on a plate as you transfer them from the pan. If they are stacked directly on top of each other they will become soggy.*

# CREPES

*This recipe is for making batter in a food processor, but you can also make the batter by hand. Sift together the flour and salt. Beat the eggs and stir in the flour and salt mixture, then beat in the milk, water, and butter. Strain.*
*Makes 12–14 crêpes*

### INGREDIENTS

*2 large eggs*
*³/4 cup (175 ml) milk*
*¹/2 cup (125 ml) water*
*3 tbsp unsalted butter, melted*
*¹/2 tsp salt*
*³/4 cup plus 2 tbsp (125 g) all-purpose flour*
*unsalted butter for the crêpe pan*

**HERB CREPES**
*Add 3 tbsp chopped fresh herbs, such as chives, parsley, tarragon, or chervil, to the batter just before making the crêpes.*

*1 Mix the eggs, milk, water, melted butter, and salt in a food processor or blender, and slowly add the flour with the machine running. Process at high speed for 1 minute. Refrigerate the batter for 1–2 hours, so that the flour particles can soften and swell.*

*2 Heat a crêpe pan over medium heat and brush the bottom with butter. When the butter just begins to smoke, remove the pan from the heat. Pour in about 3 tbsp batter. Tilt the pan to distribute the batter evenly.*

*3 Return the pan to the heat and cook the crêpe for about 1 minute. Loosen the edges gently with a spatula.*

*4 When the crêpe comes away from the pan easily, turn and cook for about 30 seconds on the other side.*

## MAKING PERFECT CREPES

- *Use a 6–7-in (15–18-cm) nonstick crêpe pan or, preferably, a seasoned pan which you use only for crêpes. Never wash the pan; just wipe clean with paper towels.*

- *While cooking, have the batter ready in a bowl, with a whisk at hand for stirring, because the flour tends to settle and the batter will need to be stirred before making each crêpe. Also have a small ladle at hand, and a plate on which to stack the finished crêpes.*

- *To prevent crêpes from sticking to the pan, make sure the pan is well seasoned and your batter is well blended so the flour does not settle.*

- *Do not panic if the first few crêpes stick. It might take that many to get the pan saturated with butter.*

- *After the first 3–4 crêpes, you will not need to brush the pan with butter every time.*

- *Turn the crêpe from the pan onto a plate, with the first (or "good") side down.*

# PREPARING VEGETABLES

A whole variety of vegetables can be stuffed with delicious fillings, cut into dippers to dunk into savory dips, or used for garnishing party platters.

Baby vegetables make the daintiest containers and are therefore ideal for finger food. Some ideas are illustrated here, and more are featured on page 25.

★

## ZUCCHINI BOATS

*1 Trim off stem ends of zucchini and discard. Blanch zucchini in boiling salted water for 1 minute. Drain and rinse under cold water.*

*2 Using a small sharp knife, cut each zucchini in half lengthwise.*

*3 With a sharp-edged teaspoon, carefully scoop out a small amount of flesh from each zucchini half.*

## CUCUMBER CUPS

*1 With a fork, score the skin of a cucumber lengthwise. Cut crosswise into ¾-in (2-cm) slices.*

*2 Using a melon baller or teaspoon, scoop out the flesh from each slice, leaving a ¼-in (5-mm) border.*

*3 Lightly salt the cups and invert on a rack to drain for about 10 minutes. Rinse before use.*

## TOMATO CUPS

*1 Using a small sharp knife, carefully cut off a thin slice from the stem ends of cherry tomatoes.*

*2 With a sharp-edged teaspoon, scoop out the seeds and flesh from the center of each tomato.*

*3 Lightly salt the hollowed-out tomatoes and invert them on a rack. Let drain briefly and rinse.*

## CARROT CURLS

*1* Cut trimmed and peeled carrots lengthwise into strips ¹/8-in (3-mm) thick.

*2* Place the carrot strips in a bowl of iced water.

*3* Place the bowl of carrot strips in the refrigerator and leave for at least 2–3 hours or overnight, until the strips become curls.

## RADISH ROSES

*1* Make a lengthwise cut down one side of a radish without slicing right through to the green top.

*2* Make 3 more similar cuts around the radish, taking care not to cut off the slices at the top.

*3* Place in a bowl of iced water and refrigerate for at least 2–3 hours. The cut sides will curl to form petals.

## SCALLION CURLS

*1* Trim the roots and most of the green parts from scallions to form pieces about 2¹/2 in (6 cm) long.

*2* Slit the bottoms so they can absorb water. Make several lengthwise cuts about 1¹/2 in (3.5 cm) long at the tops.

*3* Place in a bowl of iced water and refrigerate for at least 2–3 hours. The fringed tops will curl.

# WAYS WITH CHOCOLATE

There are many techniques involving chocolate, none of which are difficult as long as you are patient and careful. Always work in a cool place with cool hands. Melt chocolate gently – the bottom of the bowl should not touch the water in the pan or the chocolate will become overheated and burn. Stir only occasionally during melting. If you overstir, the chocolate will "seize" and stiffen into a hard lump.

★

## MELTING CHOCOLATE

## MAKING CHOCOLATE LEAVES

*Break chocolate into small pieces, place in a bowl set over a pan of simmering water, and stir with a spoon every 15 seconds until the chocolate melts.*

*1 Brush melted chocolate on the under-sides of clean, nontoxic leaves with a clean paint brush. Apply a second coat if the first was too thin. Leave to set in the refrigerator for about 30 minutes.*

*2 With cool hands, carefully peel the leaves away from the chocolate, starting from the stem end of each leaf.*

## MAKING CHOCOLATE CUPS

## FILLING CHOCOLATE CUPS

*1 Brush melted chocolate on the insides of paper or foil petit-four cases. Two layers are usually better than one. Allow the chocolate to set.*

*2 Make a small tear in the paper case and, with cool hands, carefully peel the case off each chocolate cup.*

*Put the filling of your choice (see page 125) into a pastry bag fitted with a plain or star-shaped tube. Pipe the filling neatly into each cup.*

## MAKING CHOCOLATE CURLS

Hold a bar of chocolate in your hand for a few minutes to warm and soften it slightly. Slowly pass a vegetable peeler over one of the edges to produce softly rounded curls. If the chocolate is hard, it will produce small, coarse shavings.

## CHOCOLATE-COATED FRUIT

1 Melt chocolate (see page 150), and remove the pan of water from the heat. Hold each piece of fruit by its stem or spear with a toothpick, and dip into the melted chocolate until the fruit is evenly coated.

2 Dip fruit in melted chocolate on one side only or only halfway up. This not only gives a pretty effect, it also lets the fruit stand on its uncoated side so the chocolate dries without smudging.

## MAKING & USING A PAPER PASTRY BAG

1 Cut out an 8- x 14-in (20- x 35-cm) rectangle of waxed paper. Fold over diagonally and cut to form 2 triangles. With the longest edge of 1 triangle facing you, roll the shorter side in to form a cone.

2 Holding the cone firmly with one hand, wrap the longer side over it to reinforce it. Tuck the corner of this side into the cone to secure it. The second triangle can be made into a pastry bag in the same way.

3 Fill the cone with 2–3 tbsp melted chocolate or icing and fold over the top of the cone to seal in the filling. Snip the tip of the cone and gently press the chocolate or icing through.

### ICING WITH MELTED CHOCOLATE

For a quick and easy decoration, melt chocolate and pipe it from a paper pastry bag. Here, melted white chocolate is piped in a free-flow zigzag pattern on Creamy Chocolate & Orange Bouchées (see page 125) set in rectangular chocolate cases.

# DESSERT FOUNDATIONS

These recipes are the basis of many desserts. Cut Sponge Cake into smaller shapes and top or sandwich with fruit or cream. Plain or flavored Crème Anglaise makes delicious dips, while thicker Crème Pâtissière is ideal as a filling.

★

## SPONGE CAKE

*Use this simple cake mixture as a base for petits fours, or small fancies. Butter your cake pan, line with waxed paper, then butter the paper and dust with flour.*
*Makes 1 x 8-in (20-cm) round or square cake*

### INGREDIENTS

*4 eggs, separated*
*scant 1/4 tsp cream of tartar (optional)*
*2/3 cup (150 g) superfine sugar*
*1 1/2 tsp vanilla extract (see page 156)*
*1 cup plus 2 tbsp (140 g) all-purpose flour, sifted*
*3 tbsp tepid melted butter (optional)*

*1* Beat the egg whites with a clean, dry whisk, until they begin to foam. Add a pinch of salt and the cream of tartar, if using. Beat until soft peaks form. Add 1 1/2 tbsp of the sugar and beat again until stiff peaks form. Set aside.

*2* Beat the egg yolks in another bowl. Beat in the remaining sugar, 1 tbsp at a time, until the mixture is pale yellow and leaves a ribbon trail when the whisk is lifted. Beat in the vanilla. Stir in 1/4 of the beaten egg whites.

*3* Place 1/3 of the remaining egg whites on top and sift on 1/4 of the flour. Gently fold in. Repeat with 1/3 of the remaining egg whites and 1/4 of the flour; then with 1/2 of the remaining egg whites and flour.

*4* Fold in the remaining egg whites and flour, and then fold in the melted butter, if using.

*5* Pour the batter into a prepared round or square cake pan. Tap once against the work surface to deflate large air bubbles. Bake in a 350°F (180°C) oven for 25–30 minutes.

*6* Let cool in the pan on a rack for 15–20 minutes. Invert onto another rack, remove the pan, and peel off the lining paper. Invert the cake back onto the first rack and let cool.

## CREME ANGLAISE

This is a sweet custard, traditionally used as a sauce to serve with desserts and puddings, but I like to use it as a dip for fresh fruit, either plain or with flavorings added to it (see page 134). It is important to stir the mixture well during cooking, to achieve a smooth consistency. For a truly luxurious custard, stir in a few spoonfuls of cream when cool.
Makes about 2 cups (500 ml)

### INGREDIENTS
4 large egg yolks
1/2 cup (125 g) superfine sugar
1 1/2 cups (350 ml) milk
1/2 tsp vanilla extract (see page 156)

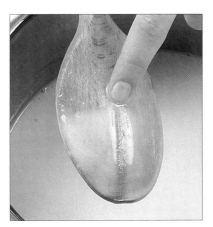

**1** Beat the egg yolks and sugar together until thick and lemon-colored. Meanwhile, heat the milk in a heavy-bottomed saucepan to simmering point, then remove from the heat.

**2** Beat the milk into the egg-yolk mixture. Pour into a pan and cook over medium-low heat, stirring. Lift the pan off the heat now and then to prevent the eggs from scrambling.

**3** Remove from the heat when the custard reaches the consistency of thick cream and coats a spoon evenly. Strain into a bowl and whisk in the vanilla extract. Let cool, then refrigerate.

## CREME PATISSIERE

This flour-based egg custard is thick enough to fill choux puffs (see pages 120–121) or to use as a sponge cake filling.
Makes about 2 cups (450 ml)

### INGREDIENTS
1 cup (250 ml) milk
1 vanilla bean, split lengthwise
3 egg yolks
5 tbsp (75 g) superfine sugar
1/4 cup (30 g) all-purpose flour, sifted

**1** Scald the milk in a pan, then add the vanilla bean, cover, and leave to infuse for about 20 minutes. Meanwhile, beat the egg yolks and sugar together until thick and lemon-colored. Whisk in the flour until just mixed.

**2** Remove the vanilla bean from the milk. Transfer the egg-yolk mixture to a heavy-bottomed saucepan and slowly pour in the milk, beating or whisking constantly, until well combined.

**3** Bring to a boil over medium heat, stirring constantly, then simmer until the mixture is very thick. Transfer to a bowl and rub the surface with a piece of chilled butter or place waxed paper on top to prevent a skin from forming.

# GARNISHES & DECORATIONS

All dishes are made instantly more appealing and appetizing when they are garnished or decorated. Even a sprig of parsley or a sprinkling of a few chopped herbs will give a dish a professional and attractive finish. Here are some simple yet stunning ideas for garnishing and decorating the savory and sweet dishes in this book. They are all eye-catching – and easy to make.

★

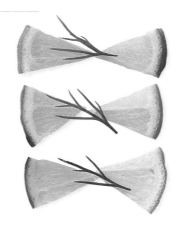

### TOMATO ROSES
*With a very sharp, small knife or a vegetable peeler, peel a continuous strip of tomato skin in a spiral. Roll up into the shape of a rose.*

### PARMESAN SHAVINGS
*Slowly pass a vegetable peeler over one of the edges of a block of fresh Parmesan cheese to produce thick shavings.*

### LIME BOWS
*Cut a lime crosswise into ¹/4-in (5-mm) slices, then cut each slice into 6 segments. Use 2 segments to make a bow and finish with a sprig of dill.*

### VEGETABLE RIBBONS
*Cut ¹/4-in (5-mm) strips from red pepper skin and from the green parts of leeks. Blanch in boiling water for about 1 minute to soften, then refresh in cold water. Use the strips to tie up phyllo pastry parcels and dolmades.*

### CARROT & CUCUMBER FENCES
*Cut carrot slices and strips of cucumber skin ¹/8 in (3 mm) thick. Trim each to about 2 in (5 cm) long. Using a sharp knife, cut out 3 sharp points at one end. Trim the other end straight across.*

## SCALLION & CAPER FLORETS

*Slice scallions into 1/2-in (1-cm) pieces. Top 3 fanned pieces with a caper.*

## ANCHOVY CURLS

*Drain and dry anchovy fillets, then wrap each fillet around a caper. Tuck a tiny red pepper diamond into each curl.*

## CHOCOLATE-COATED FRUIT

*Holding small fruit, such as strawberries, cherries, or grapes, by their stems, dip halfway into melted chocolate. Allow to set on waxed paper.*

## OLIVE CUPS & RINGS

*Make small angled cuts around the middle of a pimiento-stuffed green olive. Pull the halves apart. Cut pitted black olives into 1/4-in (5-mm) slices.*

## PICKLED GINGER ROSES

*Take 4 slices of Japanese pickled ginger. Curl 1 slice to form the center and then wrap each of the remaining pieces around it to make the shape of a rose.*

## CUCUMBER TWISTS

*Using a channel knife or stripper, cut lengthwise grooves in a cucumber. Cut crosswise into 1/8-in (3-mm) slices and cut halfway across each slice. Twist the cut ends away from each other. Tuck twists into each other to form a flower shape.*

## GHERKIN FANS

*Make 4 lengthwise cuts in small gherkins, up to 1/4 in (5 mm) from one end. Fan the slices gently from where they are joined.*

## ORANGE PEEL CURLS

*Using a channel knife or stripper, cut strips of peel to the desired length. Curl around the handle of a wooden spoon.*

## CARROT FLOWERS

*Using a channel knife or stripper, cut several lengthwise grooves in a carrot. Cut the carrot crosswise into 1/4-in (5-mm) slices to form flower shapes.*

# Author's Notes

★

## Measurements

American Standard and Metric measurements have been calculated separately. Use only one set of measures, because they are not exact equivalents. All spoon measurements are level.

## Milk

I always use low-fat milk. It doesn't affect the taste and is much healthier.

## Sugar

Unless otherwise specified, granulated sugar is used in the recipes.

## Olive oil

I always use extra-virgin olive oil, made from the first cold pressing – this should be indicated on the label of the bottle.

## Eggs

Whenever eggs are included in recipes, they are always used at room temperature.

## Juice

When lemon, lime, or orange juice is called for in a recipe, I prefer to use freshly squeezed juice, which gives a much better flavor.

## Drained yogurt

I like to use drained yogurt in some dips and sauces because it adds a smooth rich texture, and is easy to make at home. The flavor, texture, and fat content are concentrated – even nonfat yogurt will seem creamy when prepared by this method.

To make drained yogurt, place a large strainer over a bowl and line the strainer with a double thickness of cheesecloth. Spoon 2 cups (500 ml) plain nonfat yogurt into the strainer, cover, and refrigerate overnight or for several hours. The yogurt will lose up to half its volume in water into the bowl and become thick and creamy.

## Fromage blanc

This is a fresh, very soft cream cheese with the consistency of sour cream. It can be used in cooking or served with fruit.

To make fromage blanc, blend together 8 oz (250 g) nonfat cottage cheese with 3 tbsp plain nonfat yogurt until smooth.

## Dried mushrooms

The concentrated flavor of dried mushrooms adds an intense savoriness to cooked dishes, and just a small amount can transform a dish.

To rehydrate dried mushrooms, place the mushrooms in a bowl and pour boiling water over them to cover. Let stand for 15–30 minutes until softened. Place a strainer over a bowl and line the strainer with cheesecloth or paper towels. Tip the mushrooms into the strainer and let the liquid drain through; reserve the liquid for use in the recipe. Rinse the mushrooms in several changes of water, squeeze dry, and prepare according to the recipe.

## Extracts

I prefer to use extracts, which are derived from the natural product, rather than flavorings, which are made from chemically derived products.

Almond extract is made from bitter almond oil mixed with ethyl alcohol. It has an intense flavor, and only a very small amount is needed to give a strong almond taste.

Vanilla extract is a clear brown liquid with a sweet, fragrant aroma. It is made by mixing chopped vanilla beans in a solution of alcohol and water in order to extract the flavor. Vanilla extract has a concentrated flavor, and so, only a few drops are needed. Check the label before buying: if it is labeled "vanilla flavoring," or "vanilla flavored," it has been made from synthetic vanillin, which can leave a bitter aftertaste.

Remember that extracts are also sometimes called essences.

## Seasoned rice vinegar

This is the vinegar that is traditionally used to add pungency to the rice when making sushi.

To make seasoned rice vinegar, dissolve 1 tbsp sugar and 2 tsp salt in 1/4 cup (60 ml) rice vinegar. Heat over medium heat to dissolve the sugar and salt, and let cool before using.

## Baking stone

The best pizzas are made in brick ovens. A baking stone, when preheated in an oven set to 450°F (230°C), conducts heat in the same way as a brick oven floor. It is a heavy flat, round or rectangular stone, available from kitchen supply stores, and the pizza is placed directly on it in the oven.

# INDEX

★

# Acknowledgments

★

**Photographers' assistants**  Nick Allen and Sid Sideris
**Home economist**  Maddalena Bastianelli
**Typesetting**  Axis Design
**Production consultant**  Lorraine Baird
**Text film by**  Disc to Print (UK) Limited

**Author's photograph**  David Goldes (USA)

## Author's appreciation

A few of my colleagues were incredibly helpful to me as I put together this
collection. Above all, I would like to thank Anne Trager for testing many of the
recipes and for her duck and lamb terrines (pages 110–112) and marvelous fillings
for gougères (pages 50–51). Elaine Corn gave me her recipe for
Brandied Liver Pâté (page 110), and gave me much good advice about cakes.
My directions for making Gravadlax (page 104) are based on those given to
me by my friend and colleague, Susan Herrmann Loomis, while the Mincemeat
Tartlets on page 118 were inspired by Deborah Madison. Much of my inspiration
for Middle Eastern dishes, such as the meatballs (page 99), I owe to Claudia Roden.

Thanks also to Octavia Wiseman at Abner Stein Literary Agency,
and to Amy Carroll, Eric Treuillé, Jeni Wright, Shirin Patel, and
the rest of the team at Carroll & Brown.
And, as always, to my husband, Bill Grantham.